Fred A. Farrell
Glasgow's War Artist

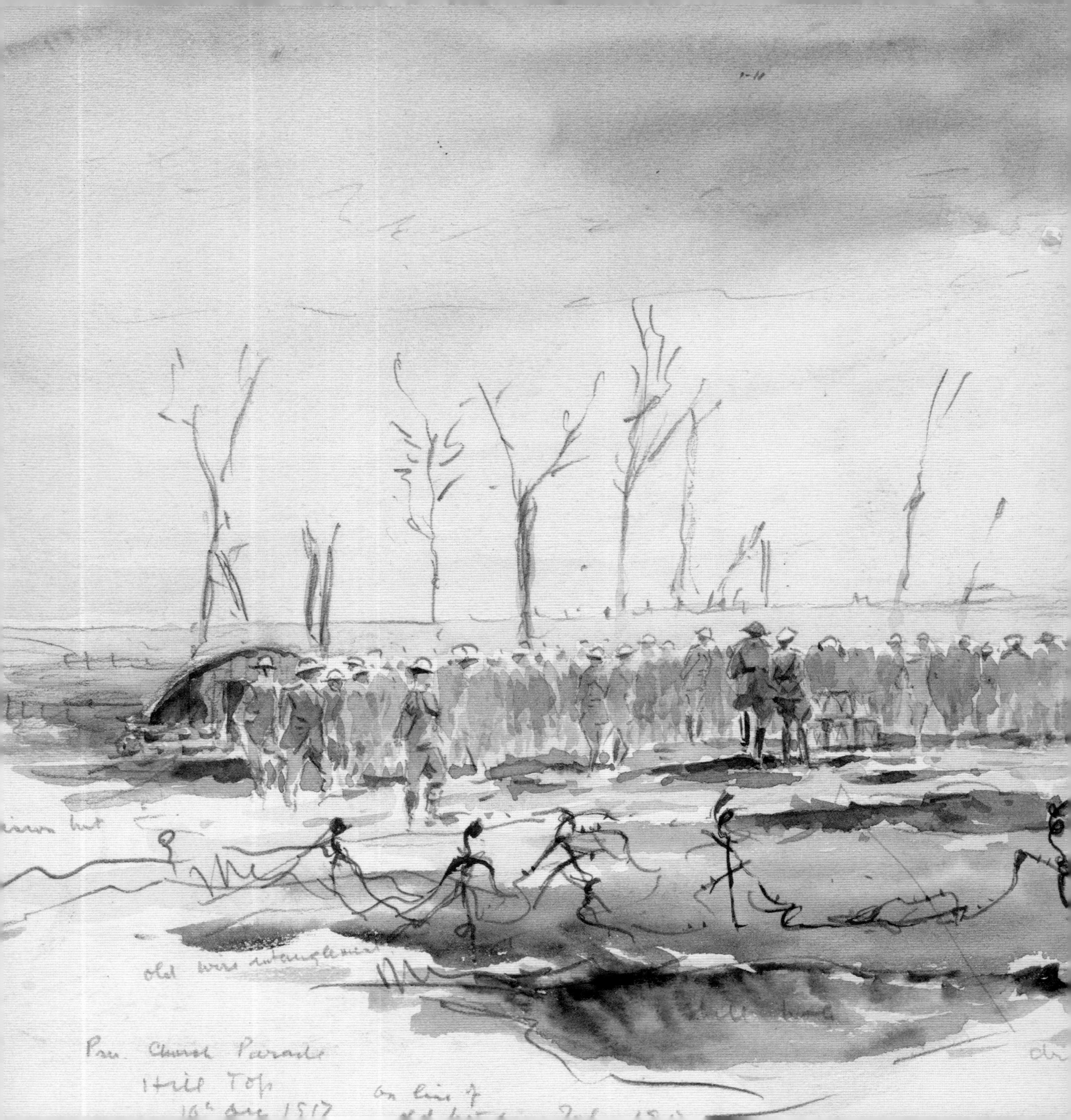
prison hut
old wire entanglement
Pan. Church Parade
Hill Top
16th Dec 1917
on line of
old line 2nd 1915

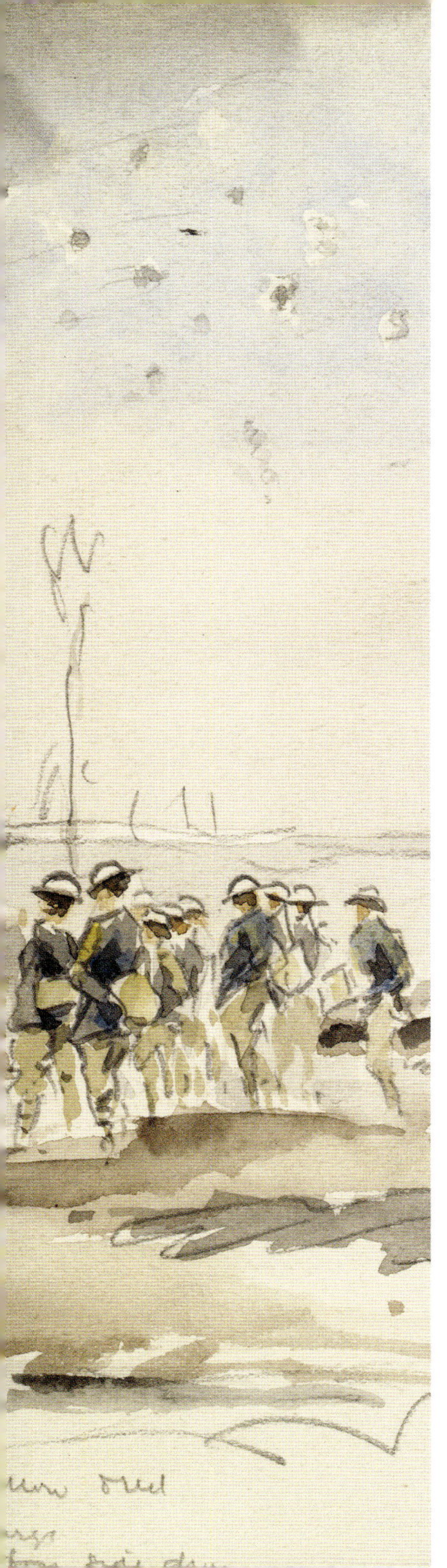

Fred A. Farrell
Glasgow's War Artist

Joanna Meacock
Fiona Hayes
Alan Greenlees
Mark Roberts

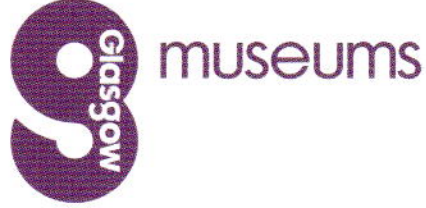

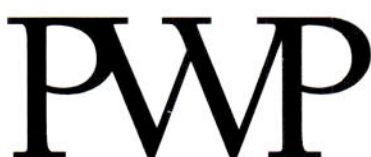

First published in 2014 by Glasgow Museums in association with Philip Wilson Publishers

Philip Wilson Publishers
an imprint of I.B.Tauris & Co Ltd
6 Salem Road
London W2 4BU

www.philip-wilson.co.uk

Distributed in the United States and Canada exclusively by Palgrave Macmillan
175 Fifth Avenue, New York NY 10010

ISBN 978-1-78130-027-5

Edited by Susan Pacitti and Helen Watkins
Editor for Philip Wilson Publishers:
David Hawkins
Additional military research by Mark Roberts
Designed by James Alexander at Jade Design
Printed and bound in Italy by Printer Trento

Typeset in Mathew Carter's 'Miller', a font based on the early 19th-century 'Scotch Roman' type which originated in the foundries of Alexander Wilson (Glasgow) and William Miller (Edinburgh).

Photography by Maureen Kinnear, Glasgow Museums, www.csgimages.org.uk
Map p. 9 based on an illustration by Sonja Taylor, Glasgow Museums

Frontispiece: *Church Parade, Hill Top* (detail), dated 16 December 1917

Acknowledgements
We are very grateful to the Friends of Glasgow Museums for a publication grant which made production of this book possible.

Thanks to Alex Robertson, Curator, Transport and Technology, who led on this project until her retirement in 2013.

We would also like to thank David Flockhart and Hazel MacLean for their help with research for this catalogue and exhibition.

This catalogue is published to accompany the exhibition *Fred A. Farrell – Glasgow's War Artist: From Home Front to Front Line in WWI*, at the People's Palace, Glasgow, 30 May – 23 November 2014.

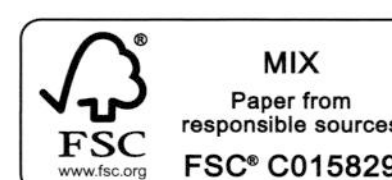

Introduction: Collecting World War I

JOANNA MEACOCK

In June 1917, Glasgow's Lord Provost, Sir Thomas Dunlop (1855–1938), wrote to John Buchan, the Director of the Department of Information at the War Office, to remind him 'of the extraordinary response this City has made in connection with the War in its contributions of men, munitions and money'.[1] Glasgow was also remarkable in its approach to collecting in relation to the war. The Pictorial Propaganda Committee, formed by the British Ministry of Information in London in July 1918, made it clear that in commissioning artists to create images of the war, its primary concern was for propaganda rather than for historical record.[2] However, in January 1917 when an exhibition of war lithographs by the American artist Joseph Pennell opened in Glasgow, Bailie Duncan Graham had predicted 'that they would be treasured even more after the war, when we will have only the sinister memory of these dreadful days'.[3] Indeed, Glasgow became one of the first cities in Britain to recognize the importance of collecting, commissioning and preserving images and objects of the war as a record for posterity, as well as a memorial to commemorate the bravery of local soldiers.

In March 1917 the *Glasgow Herald* urged museums throughout Britain to create local rolls of honour and to collect cuttings, documents, photographs and drawings recording the actions of local battalions, as well as weapons, uniforms and medals 'to bring home to future generations the real character of the struggle'.[4] By this time Glasgow Museums had already collected military memorabilia, including the nose of a German shell that had pierced HMS *Glasgow* during the Battle of Coronel off the coast of Chile on 1 November 1914. It had also acquired objects from the battlefields of France and Flanders, in addition to military badges, orders, titles and decorations. A letter to the dock workers of Liverpool from Lord Derby at the dictation of Lord Kitchener had been presented to Glasgow Museums by Glasgow oil magnate J.T. Cargill.[5]

The Corporation of Glasgow's unanimous decision to acquire 50 drawings by the Glasgow artist Fred A. Farrell of the frontline in France and Belgium and munitions factories in Glasgow, which the *Glasgow Herald* noted 'legitimately come within the category of historical documents', can be seen in the context of this pioneering approach to collecting to create a lasting national heritage.[6] In the only known photograph of Farrell (see p. 8), which appeared in the *Glasgow Bulletin*, he can be seen standing next to Bailie Carlton who represented Glasgow on the provisional national committee for the establishment of local war museums.[7] Glasgow was the only British city to commission a war artist in this way. All other commissions came from the government, Imperial War Museum or armed forces.

It was considered particularly appropriate that Farrell should document both the efforts of the

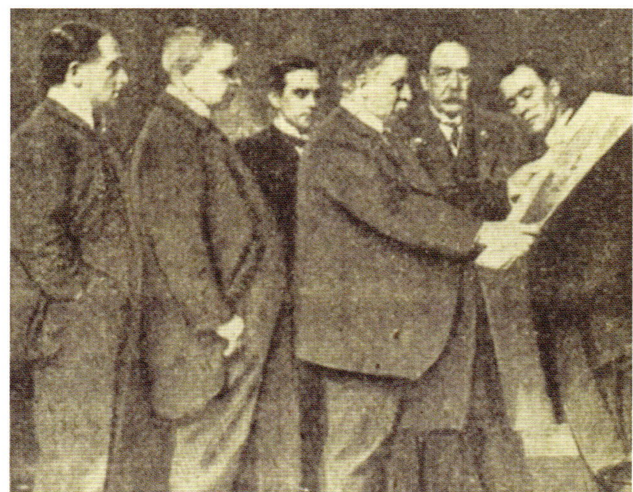

'An interesting group of critics in the City Chambers yesterday.
L. to r. – Councillor Rosslyn-Mitchell, Sir John Lindsay,
Mr F.A. Farrell, Baillie Carlton, Baillie McCulloch, and
Mr T.C.F. Brotchie.' From *The Bulletin*, 1 May 1920, p. 12.
Image © and courtesy of Glasgow City Archives.

Highland Light Infantry, which included three battalions raised in 1914 by the Corporation of Glasgow and the Glasgow Chamber of Commerce, and the 51st (Highland) Division, which contained many Glaswegians in the Territorial Force battalions of the Black Watch, Seaforth Highlanders, Gordon Highlanders and Argyll & Sutherland Highlanders.[8] In his drawings Farrell made a point of including portraits of named soldiers. In a letter to the Under Secretary for War in March 1917, the Lord Provost wrote: 'Such a collection of Drawings and Sketches applicable to our City Battalions would be very highly appreciated and prized not only by the Corporation but also, I am satisfied, by the general body of the people, who are all, more or less, related to the Members composing those Battalions.'[9]

It should be noted that Farrell played an active and tenacious role in securing the commission and, although unpaid, he obtained advantageous terms for himself that contrasted with the rather stricter contracts issued by the Ministry of Information. However, Dunlop, as Lord Provost, was key in getting the necessary permits from the War Office, Ministry of Munitions and the Admiralty for Farrell to travel to Belgium and France as well as to record the heroic home effort of women in munitions factories, shipyards and engineering works in Glasgow. In recognition of the Lord Provost's efforts, Farrell's drawings became known as the 'Sir Thomas Dunlop Collection of War Records'. This was a fitting tribute to mark Dunlop's retirement from office in November 1917, a post he had held since 1914, and which Lord Strathclyde observed had been 'national rather than municipal' in impact.[10]

In 1920 Farrell's important collection of war drawings was exhibited in the Banqueting Hall of Glasgow City Chambers to proudly mark its acquisition by the city. In the same year *The 51st (Highland) Division, War Sketches by Fred A. Farrell* was published with an introduction by the well-known journalist and writer Dr Neil Munro. But despite the importance of Glasgow's collection and Farrell's unique position among war artists, his work has been largely forgotten. At the time of national WWI centenary commemorations, this inspiring and challenging artistic record of war, both of the Front Line and Home Front, requires serious reconsideration.

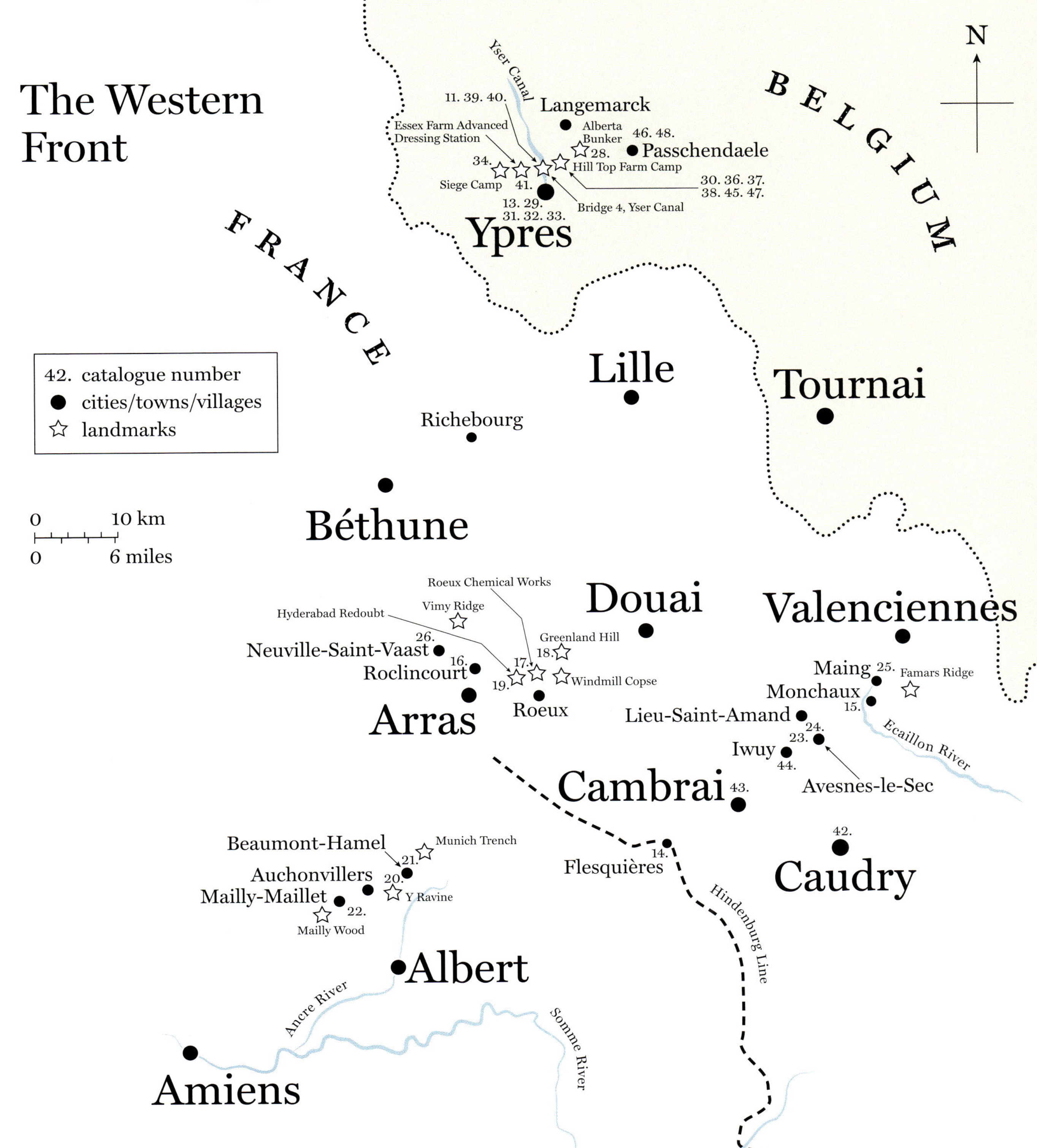

The Western Front
N
BELGIUM
FRANCE
42. catalogue number
cities/towns/villages
landmarks
0   10 km
0   6 miles
Yser Canal
11. 39. 40.
Langemarck
Essex Farm Advanced
Dressing Station
Alberta
Bunker
46. 48.
34.
28.
Passchendaele
Hill Top Farm Camp
Siege Camp   41.
30. 36. 37.
38. 45. 47.
13. 29.
Bridge 4, Yser Canal
31. 32. 33.
Ypres
Lille
Tournai
Richebourg
Béthune
Roeux Chemical Works
Vimy Ridge
Hyderabad Redoubt
Douai
Valenciennes
26.
Greenland Hill
Neuville-Saint-Vaast
18.
Maing   25.
Famars Ridge
16.
17.
Monchaux
Roclincourt
19.
Windmill Copse
15.
Lieu-Saint-Amand
Arras
Roeux
24.
Ecaillon River
23.
Iwuy
44.
Avesnes-le-Sec
Cambrai   43.
42.
Beaumont-Hamel
Munich Trench
21.
14.
Caudry
Auchonvillers
20.
Flesquières
Mailly-Maillet
Y Ravine
22.
Mailly Wood
Hindenburg Line
Albert
Ancre River
Somme River
Amiens

Fred A. Farrell: 'A fitting official and pictorial history of the War'

JOANNA MEACOCK

Early in World War I, the government recognized that pictures were an extremely powerful medium by which to influence public opinion and morale, and promote nationalism and self-sacrifice. Images were seen to have 'the qualities of downrightness and clarity' considered most effective to convey 'a fact or the summary of an argument to immense masses, educated and uneducated'.[1] However, it wasn't until May 1916 that a Picture Department was founded by Wellington House, the Propaganda Bureau established by the British government in August 1914 to disseminate views on the war to neutral and Allied nations. It was run by Ivor Nicholson of *The Times*, and through it photographs and drawings were reproduced in vast numbers and exhibited, sold and supplied as lantern slides for lectures, illustrations in newspapers and periodicals, and pictures on posters, postcards, cigarette cards, calendars and bookmarks in Britain and throughout neutral and Allied countries. This was done by means of steamship companies, diplomatic and consular representatives and other agencies. Contracts with artists were made on an *ad hoc* basis. Only from July 1918, when the Pictorial Propaganda Committee was set up by the Ministry of Information, was there a focused directive to officially sign up war artists to produce pictures for propaganda purposes.

There were three different schemes. Under Scheme 1, important paintings were acquired on an individual basis, with additional money made available at the discretion of the Committee for travelling expenses, subsistence, and cost of materials, models and studio. If it was considered appropriate for an artist to have an honorary rank in the armed forces, an allowance could also be made towards the cost of uniform.[2] Artists offered contracts on this basis included John Singer Sargent, Augustus John, Henry Tonks, William Orpen, George Clausen, D.Y. Cameron, Glyn Philpot, Walter Bayes, Wyndham Lewis and C.R.W. Nevinson. Under Scheme 2 artists were offered a salary of £300–500 per annum, plus expenses, and everything they produced would become the property of the government. Muirhead Bone, John Nash, Paul Nash, William Roberts, Stanley Spencer, James McBey and Colin Gill were given salaries in this way. Under Scheme 3, artists were given access to the Front Line and to munitions factories on the agreement that they would give the Ministry of Information first refusal of any pictures they made. All works had to be handed over to the Committee for censorship and copyright was to remain with the Committee for ever. Frank Dobson, John Everett, John Duncan Fergusson, Harold Harvey, Flora Lion and Walter Russell were among the artists approached, although many found that their works were not actually acquired in the end.[3]

In 1917, Glasgow artist Frederick Arthur Farrell (1882–1935) negotiated an unprecedented contract with the Corporation of Glasgow by which he would gift the city 50 drawings illustrating Glasgow's war effort at the Front and at home in the shipyards, engineering works and munitions factories, in exchange for assistance with expenses and in obtaining the necessary permits. Selection of the 50 was down to the City. Although Farrell carefully bargained that his works be housed in Kelvingrove Art Gallery and Museum, that the Corporation pay for their framing and that he be allowed to retain the copyright for a period of five years after the signing of peace terms in order to bring out a limited edition publication (through which he inevitably hoped to make some money), the reality was that he was unpaid, and correspondence with councillors shows that his offer was made at some personal cost.[4] Nevertheless Farrell describes the commission for which he volunteered as a glad burden, no doubt seeing any self-sacrifice as commensurate and appropriate to wartime, perhaps assuaging a young man's guilt at an early discharge. Speculation aside, Farrell's commission by the city of Glasgow remains exceptional in the history of WWI.

Where did Farrell's public-spiritedness, and yet boldness, in negotiating with the Corporation of Glasgow originate? His father, John Farrell (b. 1840/1), was a figure of some standing in the city. A former School Board Officer, from at least 1891 until 1918/19 he was Officer and then Curator of the prestigious Robert Adam-designed Trades House in Glassford Street, Glasgow, where the family also lived. Before this the family had spent about a decade in the East Indies, where three of six children were born: Ellen (b.1863/4–d. before 1891), Richard

(b.1871/2) and Thomas (b.1873/4). Mary (b.1868/9) was born in Dunning, Perthshire, circumstances having brought their mother Margaret (née Lawson, b.1840/1) back temporarily to her family home. The two youngest children, Jessie (b.1878/9) and Frederick, were both born in Glasgow; Frederick was born on 29 November 1882 at 427 New City Road.[5] Historically there were close ties between the Corporation of Glasgow and the charitable work of the Trades House, which raised considerable sums for the city's war relief funds. The city's Lord Provost, Thomas Dunlop, senior partner in Thomas Dunlop & Sons, flour merchants, shipowners and ship insurance brokers, may well have known John Farrell from his own time on the Erskine School Board in 1885–98. He certainly knew him through the Trades House, Dunlop being a member and then Deacon of the Incorporation of Bakers, and becoming President of the Association of Deacons of the Fourteen Incorporated Trades of Glasgow in 1909.[6] In a letter to Hon. Ian Macpherson MP, Under Secretary for War, Dunlop describes Fred Farrell as 'the son of a very esteemed citizen' of Glasgow.[7]

Farrell initially studied civil engineering and was apprenticed for a time to his older brother Richard, a civil engineer based in Dunoon. On 4 September 1911 Farrell married Jeannie S. McEwan in Glasgow. In this year, he certainly came within Dunlop's radar when he exhibited a portrait at the Scottish National Exhibition in Glasgow; Dunlop was the Convenor of its Scottish Modern Fine Arts Committee.[8] The address Farrell gave at this time was 175 St Vincent Street, which was probably his professional address. By 1915 the couple were living at 62 Kyle Park, Uddingston, Lanarkshire.[9] As an artist he was self-taught, although his debt to the Glasgow artist Muirhead Bone (1876–1953) is often commented on. By the start of WWI he was gaining 'a considerable reputation' as an etcher and watercolourist specializing in portraits and topographical subjects.[10] He produced views of Glasgow, Argyll, London, Bruges, Paris, the south of France, Monaco, Florence, Venice, Danzig, Poland and Macedonia.[11] He was a member of Glasgow Art Club, from whose address at 185 Bath Street he sent works for exhibition in 1917 while he was carrying out war work. He exhibited regularly at the Royal

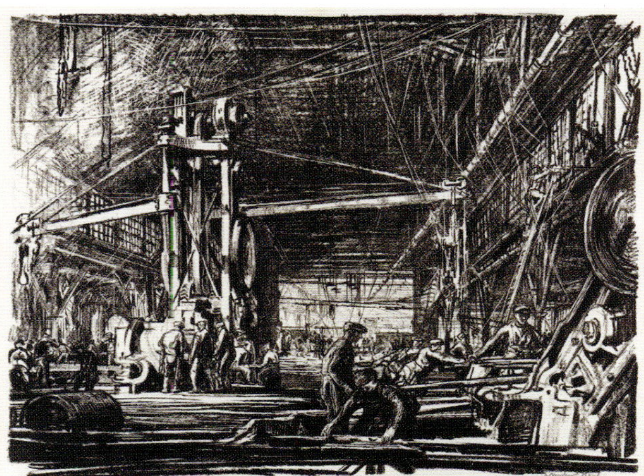

Construction Shed – Fairfield's Shipyard, c. 1917, Muirhead Bone, lithograph on paper. Given by a donor known as Mitchell, 1963, acc. no. PR.1963.11.a.

Glasgow Institute of the Fine Arts (of which Dunlop was Director 1908–14), and less frequently at the Royal Academy, Royal Scottish Academy and Walker Art Gallery in Liverpool. His topographical pictures were often reproduced in the *Glasgow Herald*.[12] The Lord Provost described him in 1917 as 'a young but distinguished local Black and White Artist'.[13]

British Army WWI Pension Records of 1914–20 show that Farrell initially enlisted as a Sapper with the Royal Engineers Railway Troops Depot on 11 December 1915, age 33 (regiment number 168933). A sapper was a military engineer, involved in bridge building, trench digging and road construction. However, Farrell was not actually called up until 13 June 1916, and was discharged less than six months later on 26 November 1916, suffering from a chronic gastric ulcer. The role of a war artist provided a route to the Front, as he was unable to be reassessed for active service until November 1917.[14]

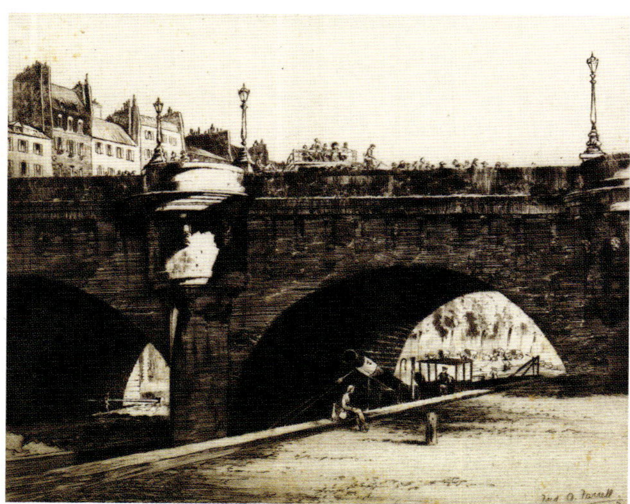

Pont Neuf, Paris, 1903, Fred A. Farrell, etching and drypoint on paper. Given by John Innes, 1920, acc. no. PR.1920.6.gf

Although some artists applied to become war artists to avoid being enlisted, many actually found themselves in imminent danger on the Front Line. C.R.W. Nevinson, who was given facilities to paint in France in June 1917 after being discharged from the Army in January 1916 because of health issues, wrote 'I have been shelled every time but once.'[15] Having seen service, Farrell was very aware of the risks. However, he was eager to be at the Front, and developed an ambitious plan involving the patronage and support of his home city of Glasgow. He may well have received advice and encouragement from Bone, who in June 1916 was the first war artist employed by Wellington House. Farrell wrote to the Under Secretary for War and to Thomas Dunlop in March 1917 requesting that he might travel to France on behalf of the Corporation to create a set of war drawings and sketches for the city's permanent collection.[16] Bone's success was a significant factor in the Corporation's enthusiasm for Farrell's proposal. In January and February 1917, 76 of Bone's drawings of 'The Western Front' had been displayed at Colnaghi & Obach's New Bond Street gallery in London to much critical acclaim. The exhibition was reported enthusiastically by the *Glasgow Herald*'s London correspondent.[17] In March and April the exhibition travelled, with additional works from the War Office and British Museum, to the National Gallery in Edinburgh and to the galleries of Messrs T. & R. Annan and Sons on Sauchiehall Street in Glasgow.[18] On 28 March, Farrell's own deeply patriotic drawing *The Spirit of Pity*, depicting Pity

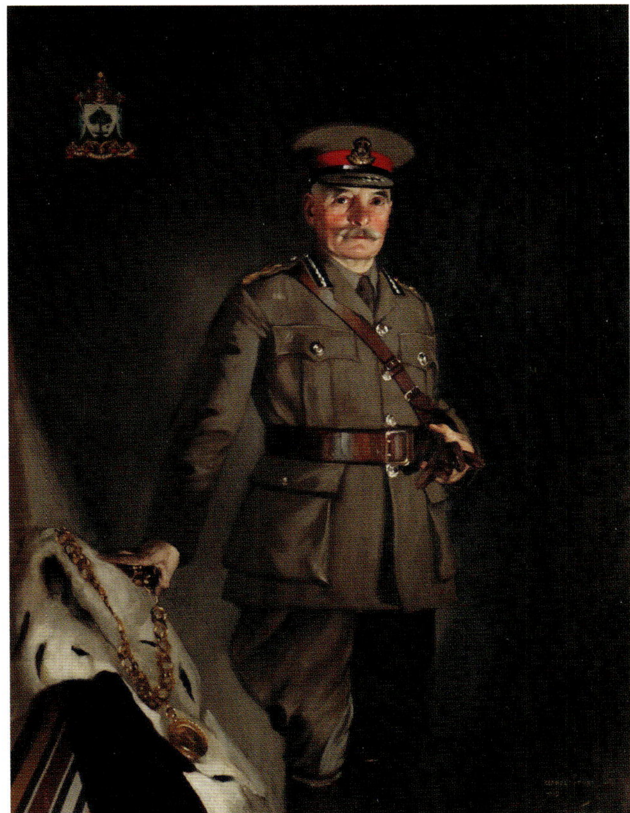

Sir Thomas Dunlop, Lord Provost of Glasgow (1914–17), 1917, George Henry, oil on canvas. Commissioned by the Corporation of Glasgow, acc. no. 1441.

as a woman rising from a land 'desolated by the arch-enemies of civilisation', with homeless refugees moving among the graves of the fallen, was exhibited at St Andrew's Hall in Glasgow. It was offered for sale in aid of the Trades House and Incorporations' War

Relief Funds, with a limited number of reproductions signed by the artist. The *Glasgow Herald* noted that, 'In view of recent happenings, Mr Farrell's drawing, so earnestly conceived and thoughtfully carried out, is singularly well timed.'[19]

Indeed, Farrell's proposition to become a war artist for the city was met with immediate approval by Glasgow's city councillors. This is in contrast to an earlier proposal by Farrell in February 1917 that the city should acquire a set of ten lithographs by the prominent American artist Joseph Pennell (1857–1926), 'which portray the dignity of engineering labour, and other industries for the making of munitions during the war'. Despite the fact that Pennell's works were championed by the persuasive author H.G. Wells, the city turned them down.[20] Without delay the Lord Provost wrote to the War Office in March 1917 to back up Farrell's case. However, Farrell was not able to obtain the necessary permissions until October 1917, and so embarked on a project to create his own record of Glasgow's munitions factories, shipyards and engineering works, the 'huge industrial apparatus that is thrusting behind' the battlefield, as Wells put it in his introduction to Pennell's catalogue.[21] Farrell wrote persuasively of his desire to document 'some of the more outstanding phases of the war work being done in the City of Glasgow and on the Clyde', and again received the full support of Dunlop, with authority swiftly granted by the Ministry of Munitions and the Admiralty.[22] Farrell is arguably at his most dynamic in these powerful drawings, which date from 1917 and 1918. Full of noise, light and movement, they capture the heat from blazing furnaces, the clanking and whirring of machinery and the sheer physical effort and sweat of the workers. They also convey an engineer's sense of structure and an artist's delight in the patterning of architecture, machinery and shells.

On the recommendation of the Department of Information, Farrell was finally attached in November 1917 to the 15th, 16th and 17th Highland Light Infantry in Flanders, where he visited sites such as Ypres, the area around which witnessed intense fighting throughout WWI, and Langemarck, where the Germans had made their first gas attack in April 1915. Although he was allowed only three weeks at the Front on this occasion, he returned to Glasgow with about 35 subjects to work up from sketches. In August 1918 he was interviewed by Alfred Yockney of the Ministry of Information, and on his recommendation Farrell returned again to the Front in late 1918, this time attached to the staff of the 51st (Highland) Division in France for a period of two months.

As a former soldier, Farrell would have been more welcome than some war artists who caused antagonism because of their ignorance of army procedure and protocol. Farrell's sketches of the Front offer a landscape filtered and mediated through personal experience and emotion.[23] They convincingly demonstrate what was so unique about an artist's vision, in contrast to a photographer's lens. Official photographers were in short supply and their images were rather limited and repetitive in depicting flat, blasted landscapes and trench scenes. Farrell's evocative drawings of men going over the top, a German prisoner being interrogated, skies lit up with gunfire and explosions, were animated and powerful. Wellington House demanded that its propaganda be restrained and detached in contrast to that of the Germans, avoiding exaggeration or extremism: 'We have determined [...] to present facts and general arguments based upon those facts'.[24] Farrell's mentor Bone was actually criticized for being too detached and distant in his war images.

Neil Munro commented on the 'truthfulness' (a historically difficult word) of Farrell's images. However, it can be said that with Farrell there was always a sense of drama, an effort to give scenes life, even those panoramas where action is presented on a small scale. Farrell travelled through France, from the Somme to the Kemmel-Arras line in the west and the Cambrai-Valenciennes line in the east, making studies of places associated with particular offensives and incidents. Battle scenes and operational meetings were reconstructed, informed by first-hand accounts from soldiers with whom he conversed. Many can be seen as patriotic and propagandist. They have active and detailed, factual-sounding titles that are eminently persuasive, such as *Battle Planes Attacking Bosche Scouting Planes with the Aid of Shrapnel Curtain Fire* (cat. no. 12) and *Breaking the Hindenburg Line* (cat. no. 14). Some are almost comic book-like in their heroic action. Others have a strange beauty, the war glimpsed objectified through an artist's eye. However, such images also stand beside grim scenes of horror, like the distressing *Hung Up!* (cat. no. 50), and poignant depictions of graves, devastated landscapes and destroyed churches that leave the viewer disturbed and questioning. But there is always hope, with scenes of renewal and activity amid the desolation. Unfortunately no diaries or letters are known to exist that might shed light on Farrell's experiences at the Front and how he actually felt about the war as he witnessed it first hand.

Above all this collection documents Glasgow's war, its men and women, at home and on the Front Line. It highlights the multi-faceted nature of war, its offensives, horrors and personal sacrifices. They are executed by a self-made artist, a former soldier with first-hand experience of the Front, who with an exceptional public-spiritedness gifted the collection to Glasgow as part of a national war effort and as a unique record for the city. As Thomas Dunlop wrote, they are indeed 'a fitting official and pictorial history of the War'.[25]

The Home Front: 'While it was not ours to fight – we worked.'[1]

FIONA HAYES

When war was declared on 4 August 1914, few people could have imagined how much their home and daily life would be affected or that they would become part of the effort to win the war. No home was untouched by World War I. The term 'Home Front' was first used during this time in recognition that the effects of war reached far beyond the Front Line into the everyday lives of the civilian population. People at home were encouraged by the government to support the war as their patriotic duty, and the whole country seemed to be mobilized to contribute to the 'Final Victory'.

It comes as no surprise that war artists depicted this aspect of the war effort as part of their record of WWI. For Farrell, it meant recording the Clydeside munitions factories and workers in 1917 while he waited for permission to travel to the Front Line, and again in 1918 after his return.

Ten of the 50 drawings selected for the Corporation of Glasgow's art collection depict Glasgow's Home Front. Two aspects dominate the drawings on this subject – the scale and scope of munitions work and the fact that women make up most of the workforce. These drawings bring an immediate sense of the heat, noise and scale and urgency of munitions work. The human figures are part of a huge machine producing armaments for the Front Line; they are all essential components yet are dwarfed by the scale of the enterprise. Whether it is in the purpose-built National Projectile Factory at Cardonald or the established workshops and shipyard sites where production has been converted to war work, the viewer is drawn into what it was like to work in munitions.

These images record that the city 'did its bit'. But not everyone in Glasgow bought into the patriotic fervour, and it is pertinent to note that this is also the period of Red Clydeside, when Glasgow was the centre of increasing radical left-wing political grassroots movements and anti-war agitation. The workers in the yards and factories would have known of men such as John Maclean, teacher and British Socialist Party leader, who denounced the war as a capitalist exercise pitting worker against worker. The 'Shell Scandal' of 1915 highlighted that Britain just did not have enough shells to fight the new type of war. This type of ammunition needed to be produced on an unprecedented scale to bring any hope of victory. As a result, the Ministry of Munitions was created to co-ordinate the production and distribution of munitions. In Glasgow the energetic William Weir, director of engineering firm G. and J. Weir, was appointed Director of Munitions for Scotland. He proposed the Glasgow Shell Scheme as the most effective and efficient means to do this – local businesses were to run the munitions work on behalf of the Ministry's national scheme so that they could produce the equipment and ammunitions needed on the Front Line. The Ministry would provide firms with financial assistance to

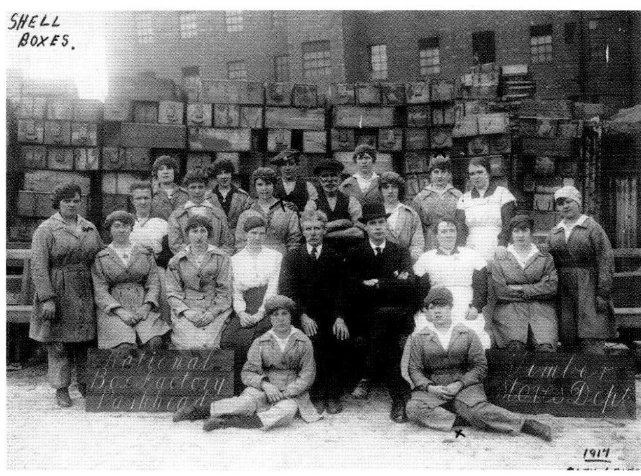

Workers at the National Box Factory Parkhead in Glasgow's East End in front of a wall of wooden boxes used to transport shells to the Front Line. Acc. no. GMA.1540.2007.1.

develop their munitions work. From a slow start new factories were built, and production in existing forges, workshops and yards was converted to munitions work.

Glasgow's shipyards and heavy engineering firms quickly became an important part of the war effort. The materials, skills, labour and transport infrastructure were already in place and could be turned to munitions work. So, although armaments were not a product associated with Glasgow's industries at the outbreak of the war, by Armistice in 1918 they were a major part of the city's output.

The government funded the creation of 15 National Projectile Factories (NPF) to make heavy shells; six of them were sited in and around Glasgow. Established between 1915 and 1916, they were run by three of the companies behind the Glasgow Shell Scheme, and some were named after battles on the Western Front.

William Beardmore & Co. Ltd. managed three:
- National Projectile Factory Cardonald, built in Craigton, Glasgow;
- National Projectile Factory Mile End, set up in Grant's Mill, an existing cotton mill building in the east end of Glasgow; and
- National Projectile Factory Mossend, built near Bellshill, Lanarkshire.

Babcock & Wilcox Ltd built and managed two in Renfrewshire:
- National Projectile Factory Renfrew – Aisne; and
- National Projectile Factory Renfrew – Ypres.

G. & J. Weir Ltd. managed one:
- National Projectile Factory Cathcart, built on Weir's Holm Foundry site in Glasgow. Parts of the factory were named 'Albert' and 'Flanders'.

Other companies in the Glasgow Shell Scheme included the North British Locomotive Co., which ran the 'Mons' and 'Marne' factories in Springburn, Glasgow, and Mechans Ltd who named their factory 'Edith Cavell' after the British nurse shot by the Germans for helping Allied soldiers escape from occupied Belgium.

Separate factories filled shells with explosives. In Glasgow, the National Filling Factory Cardonald was near the Cardonald NPF. Sited 10 miles outside the city at Erskine, but well served by rail links, was the huge National Filling Factory Georgetown (also known as the Scottish Filling Factory).

Other factories made the fuses which detonated shells. Singer's, the sewing machine manufacturers, ran Combles Fuse Factory in Clydebank, and Beardmore's ran the Temple Fuse Factory in Anniesland, Glasgow. The National Box Factory in Parkhead made the crates that carried the shells to the Front Line. Most of the workers in these factories were women.

As can be seen from Farrell's works, the range of war equipment produced on the Clyde was large and varied – submarines, tanks, pumps, guns and the all-important shells, which were made in different sizes. Of the Home Front works, the Cardonald National Projectile Factory (NPF) is the subject of more of his drawings than any other factory (see cat. nos. 4–8). The booklet *Souvenir of Cardonald National Projectile Factory* produced in 1919 provides some context for the drawings Farrell made there. In the style of the time the booklet can be seen as a piece of propaganda, but it does show that within a fortnight of opening the factory was operating a day and a night shift. It records that in March 1917, 2,893 women were employed alongside 1,500 men and 113 boys with the factory producing 74,202 eight-inch shells that month.[2] The factory made the six-inch chemical shell 'which played so large a part in the final phase of hostilities',[3] and was the subject of one of Farrell's 1918 works (see cat. no. 5). The booklet boasts that production increased from 6,488 six-inch shells per month in April 1918 to 74,995 in October 1918. The Cardonald NPF also provided a canteen where workers could buy breakfast and dinner.

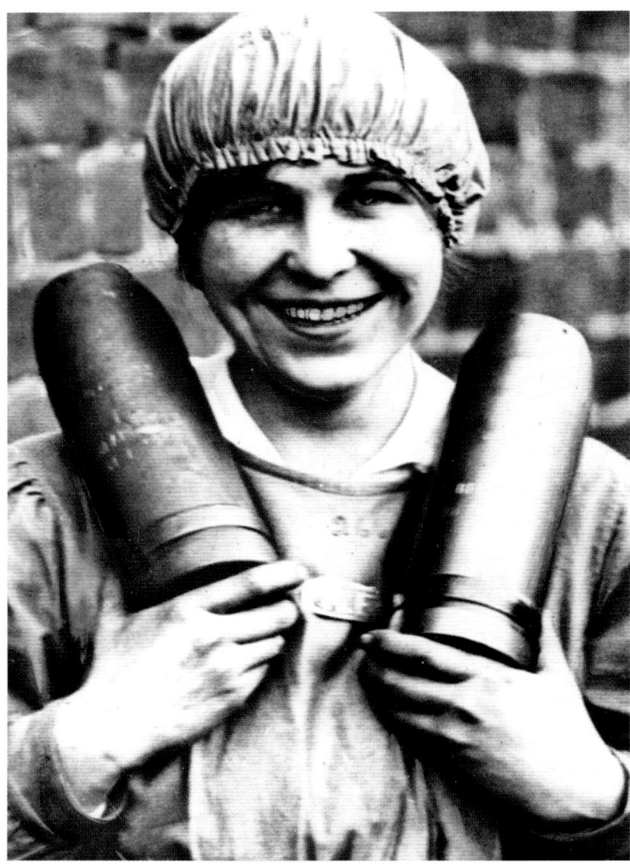

This young woman worked at one of William Beardmore & Co.'s sites in 1915. Her smiling face represents the public image of the munitions worker doing her bit. Acc. no. TEMP.2039.172.

The government had turned to the country's women to fill the labour shortage as the numbers of men who enlisted or, from January 1916, were conscripted grew. These factories relied on female workers, and everywhere women could be seen in roles that were usually designated as men's.

Many women signed up for munitions work – it was not only patriotic, but also well paid. The government regulated women's munitions work wages and they earned a minimum of 20 shillings a week. However, it was hard, dangerous, physical work with long hours on continuous repetitive tasks. The British class system was brought into sharp relief too – the supervisory and welfare jobs were the province of middle-class women, whereas the work on the factory floor was carried out by working-class women. By the end of the war women were involved in all stages of production, from forging and casting to machining, packing and filling.

What we cannot deduce from Farrell's drawings is what life was like for the women and men he portrayed. When private landlords sharply increased rents in the months after war was declared in 1915, local working-class women organized rent strikes which spread throughout the city. At public demonstrations children carried placards that likened the city's landlords to 'Huns', the German enemy. When the protest threatened to spread further and disrupt the war work in the yards, the government quickly introduced the Rent Restriction Act of 1915 which kept rents at a pre-war level for the duration of the war.

Workers would also have had to deal with food shortages as the war progressed, making it a challenge to get enough nutritious food to enable them to perform the heavy physical tasks shown in these drawings. Staple food such as bread was becoming more expensive and scarce. That other staple of the working class Glaswegian's diet, the potato, was also in short supply in 1917. By the early twentieth century, Britain was importing many staple foodstuffs, such as wheat, from her dominions and colonies. German U-boats' blockade of Britain's ports and shipping lines from 1917 cut off this supply. After trying to encourage people to ration their own food, a national system of rationing was introduced in February 1918.

The Armistice was signed on 11 November 1918 and there was no longer need for munitions on the same scale. The surviving soldiers returned from the Front Line, and women were expected to step aside from their wartime working roles. There were new uses for some purpose-built factories. Wallace Farm Implements Ltd bought Cardonald NPF to make a three-wheeled tractor which was known as the 'Glasgow' tractor.

The author of the *Souvenir of Cardonald National Projectile Factory* summed it up – 'Our work in the War is done. We have answered the call of the troops for ammunition, and the task which has been given us, and in which we set out with such determination, has been accomplished. Soon it will be but memory. But there will ever remain with us the knowledge that while it was not ours to fight – we worked.'[4]

Farrell's Home Front works record that period towards the end of the war when munitions production was at its peak. He recorded Glasgow's women and men engaged in 'some of the more outstanding phases of the war work being done in the City of Glasgow and on the Clyde'.[5] These drawings ensure that the memory of Glasgow's Home Front contribution to the war has not been lost.

Fred A. Farrell: 'Truthful representations of the character and aspect of modern war'

ALAN GREENLEES

Mr. Fred. A. Farrell, the Scottish etcher ... took the opportunity of traversing all the ground covered by the Highlanders in France and Flanders from Beaumont-Hamel onwards ... and his sketches ... associated with incidents of these battles as minutely described by actual participants on the spot, wonderfully reproduce the aspect and evoke the emotions of high historic hours.

Neil Munro, introduction to *The 51st (Highland) Division, War Sketches by Fred A. Farrell*

Fred A. Farrell made two forays to the Western Front as a war artist. In late November or early December 1917 he went to Flanders (northern Belgium) where he spent about three weeks attached to battalions of the Highland Light Infantry (HLI) regiment in the 32nd Division. His second visit was to France in late 1918 where he was attached to the staff of the 51st (Highland) Division for two months. Farrell may have witnessed some fighting first hand but he could not have witnessed all the scenes he depicted, so some are reconstructions. He retraced the steps of the 51st in France and Flanders from Beaumont-Hamel onwards, making sketches of the actual battlefields. He met eyewitnesses and heard their accounts, often including the men in his drawings.

No written account of Farrell's movements around the Front is known to exist. We are therefore heavily reliant on the annotations on the pictures themselves for information about what they show. Sometimes his writing is hard to decipher. Farrell appears to have made quick sketches at the scene and developed them into finished watercolours later. Dates can be confusing – sometimes referring to the date a sketch was started, a later date at which it was finished, or the date of an event Farrell was recreating. Some of the annotations have clearly been made as a reminder to himself. In *The Hyderabad Redoubt* (cat. no. 19) his notes include the colours 'blue', 'grey', 'greyish', 'brown' and 'yellow' along with features of the landscape, 'barbed wire', 'shell hole' and 'snow'. There is also a little sketch plan of the defences. The annotations for *Church Parade, Hill Top* (cat. no. 47) include a small sketch detailing the arrangement of the piled drums used as an altar. Another source of information is Farrell's book *The 51st (Highland) Division, War Sketches by Fred A. Farrell*. It features 16 of the images in this book and their descriptions provide further valuable clues to the stories behind the pictures.

At the outbreak of war the British Army consisted of two main parts: the regular army and the Territorial Force. The regular army, made up of full-time professionals, was well equipped and trained but relatively small. The Territorial Force, intended for home defence, was made up of part-time paid volunteers. Realizing that the size of the army needed to increase dramatically, the Secretary of State for War, Field Marshal Kitchener, recruited a new army of volunteers to fight abroad for the duration of the war; they were known as Kitchener's New Army. Conscription was introduced in 1916 when the flow of volunteers dwindled and the distinctions between different parts of the army became blurred. The units depicted by Farrell were all from either the New Army or the Territorial Force.

Ten of the works in this catalogue feature the 15th, 16th and 17th battalions of the Highland Light Infantry. Battalions were the building blocks of the army – at full strength a battalion numbered about 1,000 men, but later in the war it was common for an infantry battalion to be well under half strength. Three New Army battalions of the HLI, the 15th, 16th and 17th, were raised in Glasgow, and were subtitled the 1st, 2nd and 3rd Glasgow. The original name of the 15th HLI (nicknamed the 'Boozy First'), was the 'Glasgow Tramways Battalion' as most of their recruits worked for Glasgow Corporation Tramways. The 16th HLI were originally called the 'Glasgow Boys' Brigade Battalion', nicknamed the 'Holy Second' as most of their recruits were former members of the Boys' Brigade. The raising of the 15th and 16th HLI was arranged and funded by the Corporation of Glasgow. The 17th HLI (the 'Saintly Third'), whose original recruits were mainly white collar workers from local businesses and students from the Royal Technical College, Glasgow, was raised by Glasgow Chamber of Commerce and originally called the 'Glasgow Commercials'. (The 17th were also known as the 'Featherbeds' after their tents at their training camp in Ayrshire were destroyed in a storm and they were moved to comfortable billets in nearby Troon.)

Farrell's first trip was to the Ypres salient in Flanders, where he spent about three weeks attached to the 15th, 16th and 17th HLI in late 1917. Desperate attempts were made to break the German stranglehold on the salient. The Third Battle of Ypres (also known as the Battle of Passchendaele) concluded on 10 November 1917. However, in the early hours of 2 December 1917, a further large-scale operation was conducted on the Passchendaele Ridge under the cover of darkness. The 15th, 16th and 17th HLI were among the battalions taking part. The attack was a failure, and from the 17th HLI alone, 48 soldiers were killed, 135 wounded, and 13 listed as missing. By 10 December the 17th HLI had been moved to Hill Top Farm, a camp on a slight rise north east of Ypres. Farrell recorded life there, depicting a religious service (cat. no. 47), mobile cookers preparing welcome hot food (cat. no. 36) and the view from the camp (cat. no. 45). He also made a portrait of Quartermaster Lieut James Kelly (cat. no. 37). Farrell showed the officers preparing for their return to the Front (cat. no. 30) and the troops moving out (cat. no. 38). Soldiers regularly rotated between the trenches and camps away from the Front Line, normally spending only a few days at a time at the Front. A common feature of the pictures are the gasmasks which the soldiers carry on their chests in square webbing bags. Chemical weapons were used extensively by both sides on the Western Front.

Farrell then travelled to Passchendaele Ridge where he recorded the fresh graves of soldiers from the 16th HLI killed on 2 December in *Graves* (cat. no. 46). He also portrayed the shattered landscape in *Ypres Salient 1917 – Behind Passchendaele* (cat. no. 48).

In late 1918, Farrell's second visit took him to France where he spent two months attached to the staff of the 51st (Highland) Division – the 51st feature in 12 of the works in this catalogue. A division comprised three or four brigades, each of four battalions (reduced to three in 1918). Artillery, engineer, transport, medical and veterinary units were attached to a division to provide specialist support. Despite the 'Highland' designation, many of the men serving in the 51st were from Glasgow. The territorial units of the Black Watch, Seaforth, Cameron, Gordon and Argyll & Sutherland Highlanders from across Scotland had been reinforced by volunteers and conscripted men. The pioneer battalion was from the Royal Scots. From April 1915 to January 1916 the 6th Cameronians (Scottish Rifles), who were a Glasgow Territorial unit, and some units from Lancashire (the King's Own (Royal Lancaster), the King's (Liverpool), the Lancashire Fusiliers and the Loyal North Lancashire) were part of the 51st Division. The Highland regiments wore kilts while the Cameronians and the Royal Scots did not. The division's early nickname, 'Harper's Duds', was a reference to their commander, General Harper, and to the limited success of the division in its early battles. This nickname was swiftly dropped as the war progressed and they established a reputation as a hard-fighting formation. Reputedly, a captured German document placed the 51st at the top of a list of British troops most to be feared.

In *Breaking the Hindenburg Line* (cat. no. 14), Farrell depicts part of the Battle of Cambrai, during November 1917. The 6th Gordons and 6th Seaforths are advancing upon Flesquières behind rows of tanks. General Harper's tank co-operation tactics were controversial and are still debated by historians.

4th Gordons Clearing Crest, Greenland Hill (cat. no. 18) shows soldiers walking in lines abreast, but by this stage of the conflict an attack would not usually have been mounted in that formation. Earlier in the war, when soldiers went 'over the top' and advanced towards the enemy walking abreast in long lines, they were quickly mown down by enemy fire. The lessons learnt on the Somme led to the introduction of new tactics. Advancing behind a 'creeping barrage' of shellfire, waves of men rushed forward, using any available cover, dashing from one shell hole to another and giving each other covering fire. They used rifles, rifle grenades, Lewis guns and hand grenades to storm German positions and were supported by artillery, trench mortars and heavy machine guns. Reinforcements followed in short columns known as 'worms', mopping up any resistance. Further waves secured captured territory and brought fresh supplies.

Combat on the Western Front was not confined to the big set-piece battles. Both sides conducted trench raids, involving anything from a couple of men to over a hundred. They were done stealthily at night, using knives, clubs and knuckledusters

Right: *The Hyderabad Redoubt* (detail), dated 18 July 1919.

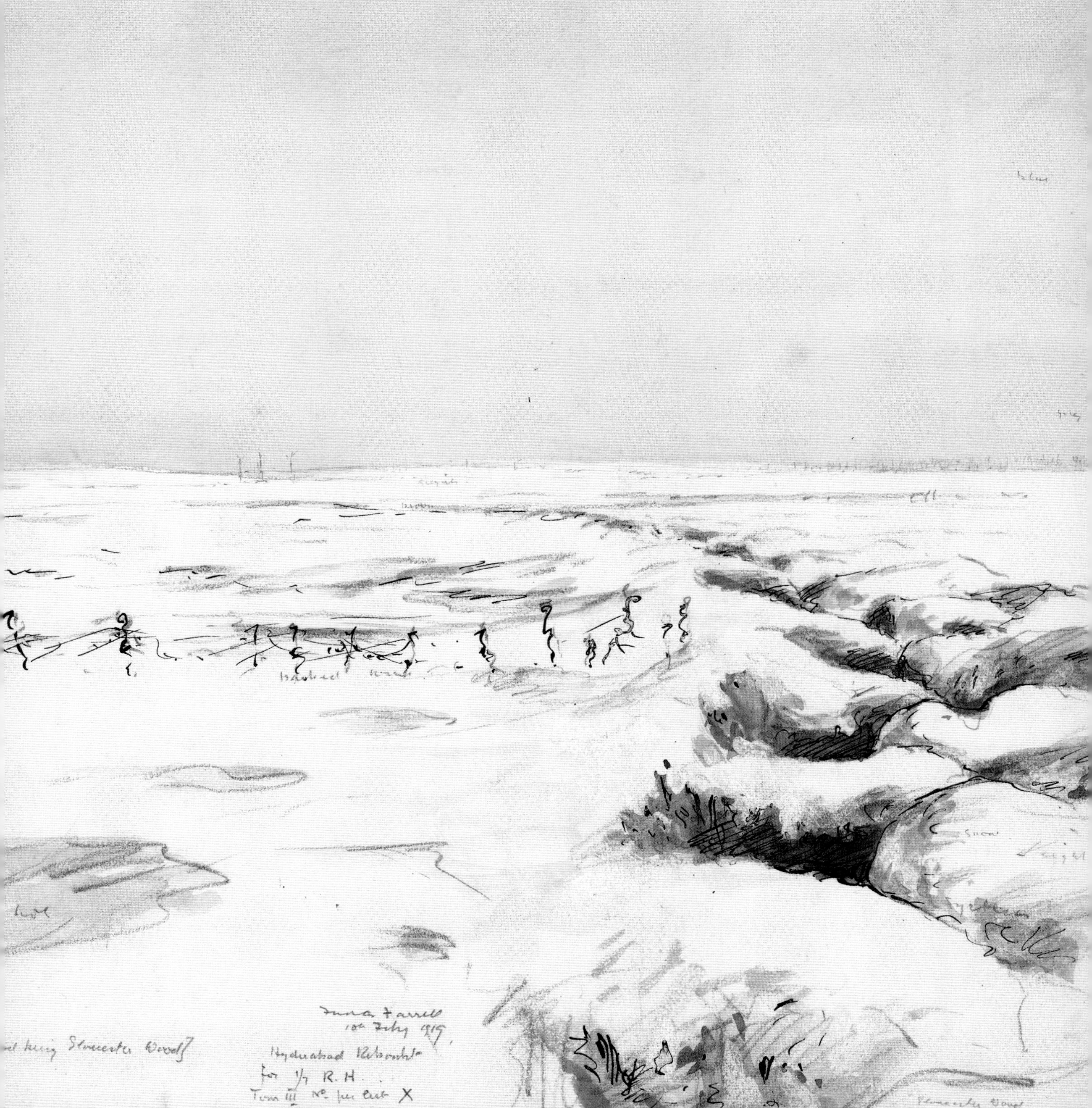

Barbed Wire
Anna Farrell
10th Feby 1919.
Hyderabad Redoubt
for 1/7 R.H.
Turn III No. per cut X
...king Gloucester Wood

to avoid gunfire alerting the enemy. Soldiers were known to remove their kilts for raids and wear only the khaki apron cover, so as to be unencumbered. The purpose was to take prisoners for interrogation, capture or destroy valuable weapons and equipment and to maintain 'fighting spirit' whilst wearing down the enemy. A witness recalled the 17th HLI returning from a raid:

The 17th were commonly known as the Raiders, and most excellent they were at the job – the Hun had a holy horror of the men from Glasgow … The big drummer and a little corporal of the H.L.I. … asked me not to question them as to details of the raid, as some very dirty work took place across the way! I expect it did from the look in their eye and the happy way they handled their clubs.

Later in the war, larger raids involving whole battalions were carried out in daylight, as shown in *Daylight Raid by the 6th Gordons at Roclincourt* (cat. no. 16). Stealth was replaced by an artillery 'box barrage' which cut off a section of enemy trenches on three sides during an attack. Daylight raids were known as 'flying matinees'.

A recurring feature of Farrell's pictures are the stretcher bearers, seen in cat. nos. 14, 17, 21 and 41. Casualties received first aid at the Front Line and were sent to Bearer Relay Posts to be collected by the Field Ambulances. These were not vehicles, but units of the Royal Army Medical Corps who evacuated casualties using stretcher bearers, horse-drawn ambulances and motorized ambulances. At Dressing Stations, which were still within range of enemy artillery fire, casualties had their wounds dressed and emergency surgery could be done. The wounded were then transferred to Casualty Clearing Stations, small hospitals in tents or huts just beyond the line of fire. Patients remained until they were well enough to move to the larger Base Hospitals or return to their units.

It is beyond the scope of this publication to describe the many battles fought by the soldiers Farrell depicted, let alone to convey the horrors they had to endure. Farrell himself was restricted by the censors, who forbade the depiction of dead soldiers. With one known exception (cat. no. 50), he showed helmets scattered on the ground to symbolize bodies. Working within these limitations he used his own experiences, combined with first-hand accounts, to create a compelling eyewitness portrayal of the war.

If in Mr Farrell's sketches there be little to recall … any of those magnificently imagined but quite untruthful canvases that … make war seem romantic and beautiful, it is because the greatest war in history was marked by no scenic splendour, thrilling panoramic effects, or great isolated incidents capable of representation by theatrical posturing afterwards before the easel … Mr Farrell's sketches will be recognized by all who were in France and Flanders in the fighting lines as truthful representations of the character and aspect of modern war.
Neil Munro, introduction to *The 51st (Highland) Division, War Sketches by Fred A. Farrell*

Right: *Intelligence Officer's Shelter: Prisoner Awaiting Re-examination* (detail), undated.

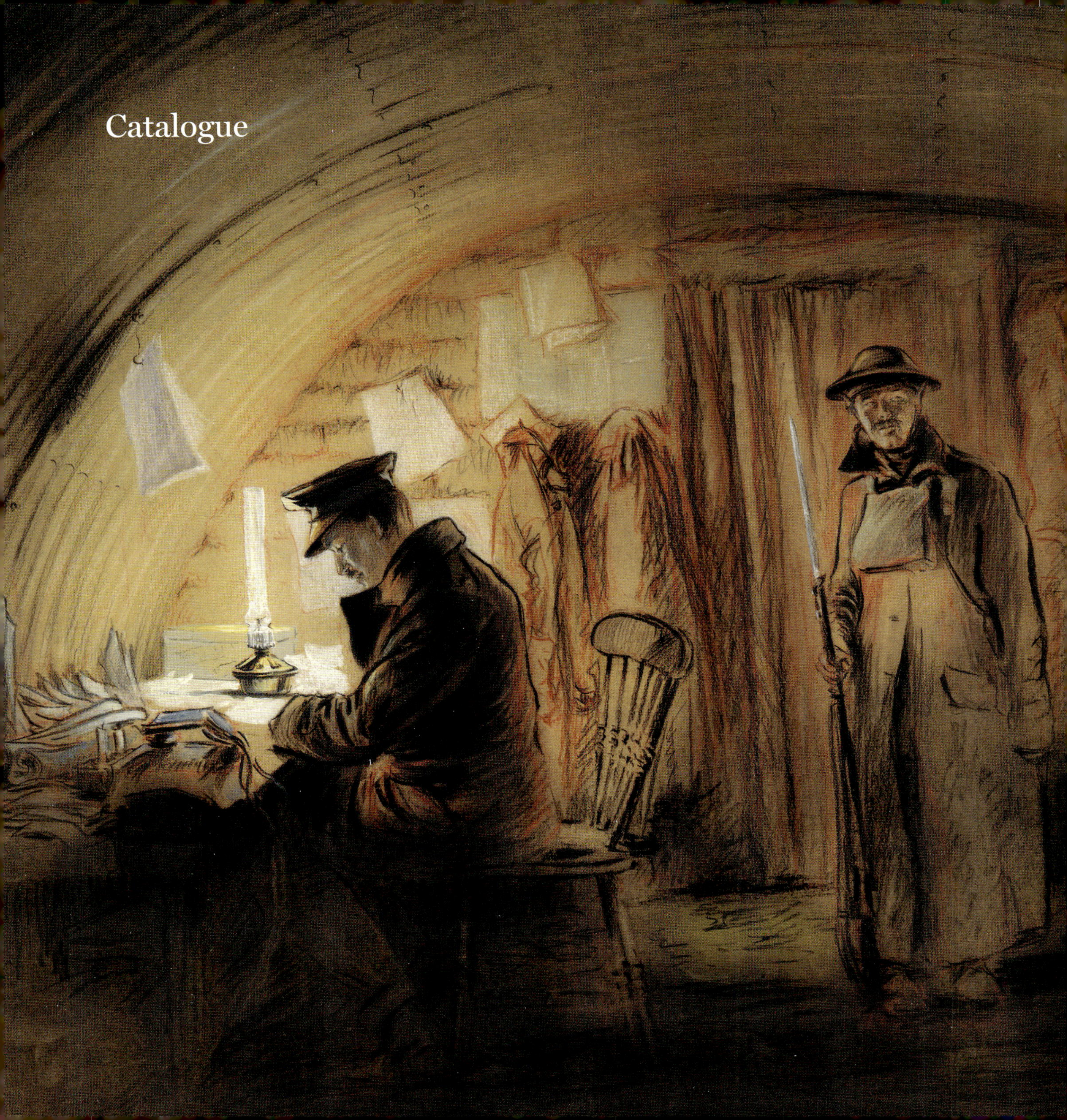
Catalogue

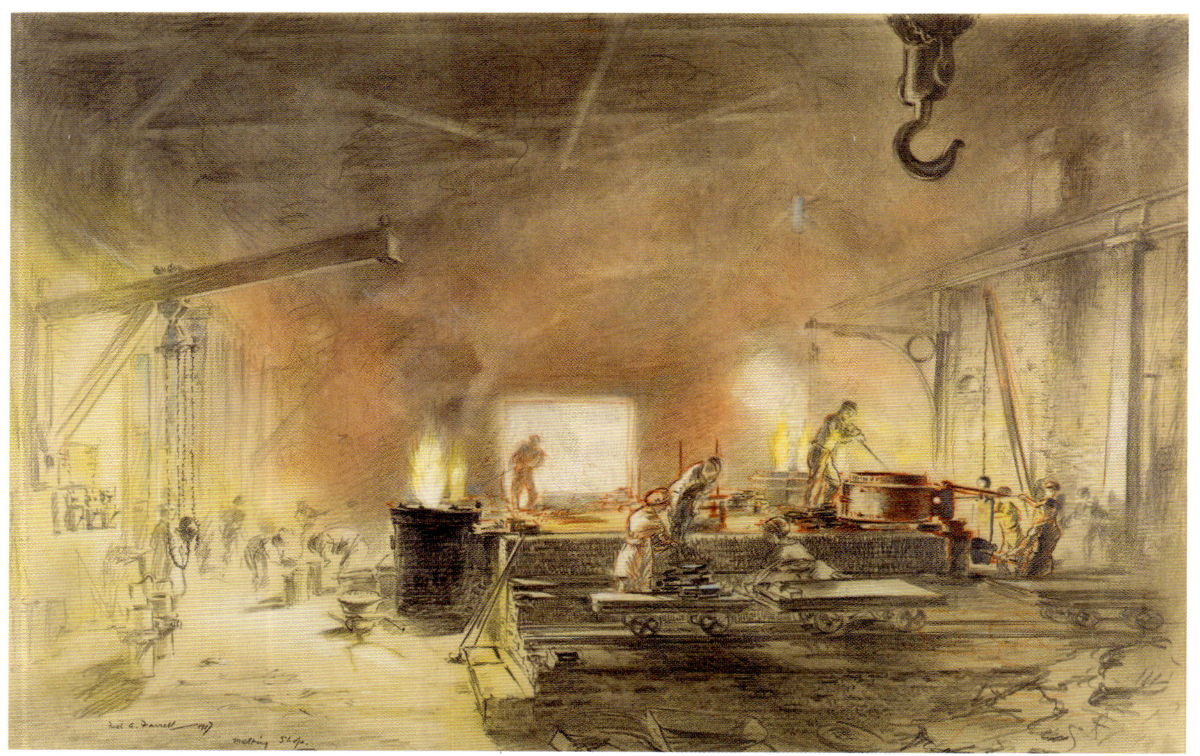

1

Melting Shop

Signed and dated 'Fred A. Farrell 1917'
Inscription: 'Melting Shop.'
Watercolour, pencil and chalk on paper
PR.1921.23.t

The process of making guns and shells began in the melting shops. Metal was melted in furnaces then transported by overhead rails and poured into wooden moulds in casting pits dug into the 'greensand' floors. Here Farrell shows iron ingots being brought to the furnaces on a mini railway. He skilfully suggests the extreme heat of the melting shop through the brilliant yellow-white glare at the left, through which figures appear almost mirage-like. Women work alongside men. Beardmore's National Projectile Factory Mossend was the first in Britain to employ women as 'tongers', a physically demanding job where tongs suspended from overhead wires were used to pull white-hot, molten ingots from the furnaces.

Note: The City of Glasgow accepted the proposed gift of 50 war drawings by Fred A. Farrell in October 1917, and the works were received into Glasgow Museums' collection in 1919.

The inscriptions included in this catalogue are literal transcriptions, reflecting Farrell's original spelling.

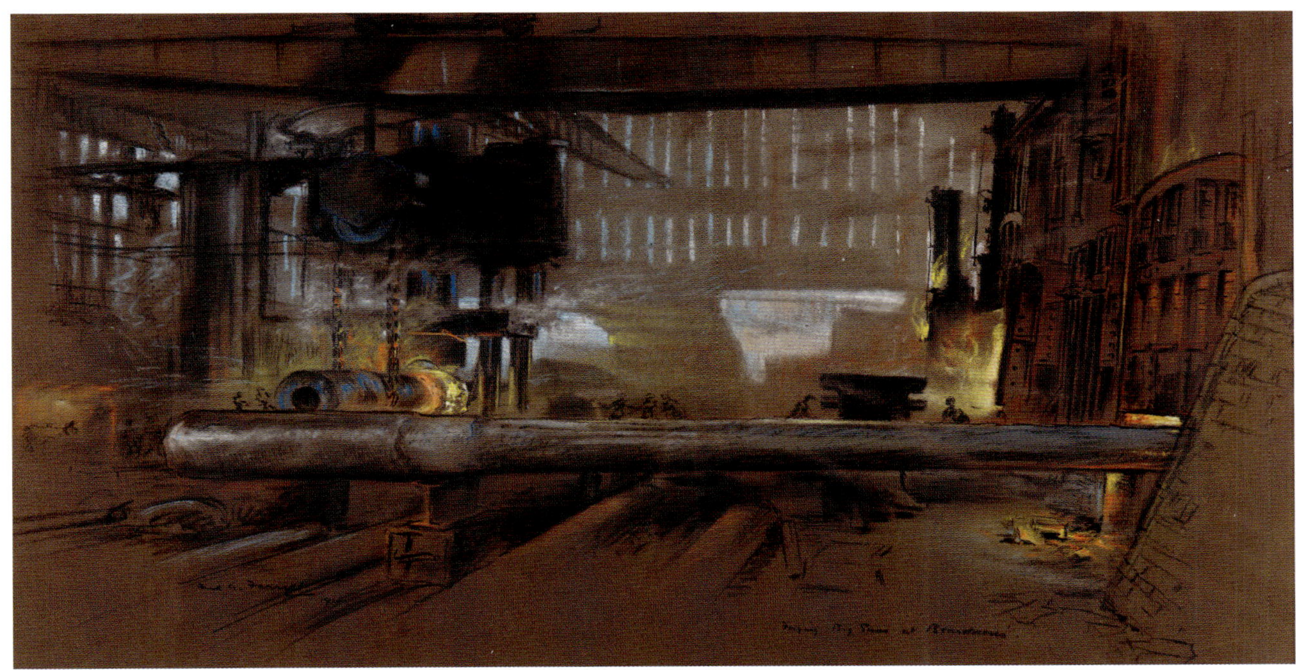

2

Forging Big Guns at Beardmore's

Signed and dated: 'Fred A. Farrell 1918.'
Inscription: 'Forging Big Guns at
Beardmores'
Chalk and crayon on paper
PR.1921.23.av

Here, following casting, massive guns for a warship are being heated and tempered to harden the barrels so they can withstand the explosive force of being fired. Heavy lifting cranes are used to lift the weight of the guns. Large guns were made both at Beardmore's Parkhead Forge and its Naval Construction Works at Dalmuir in Clydebank.

A heavy hammer driven by shafts beats the gun in the background. Farrell shows his skill as a colourist, the merest touches of blue, yellow and orange giving volume and substance, suggesting light glinting on metal and the heat from the forging ovens.

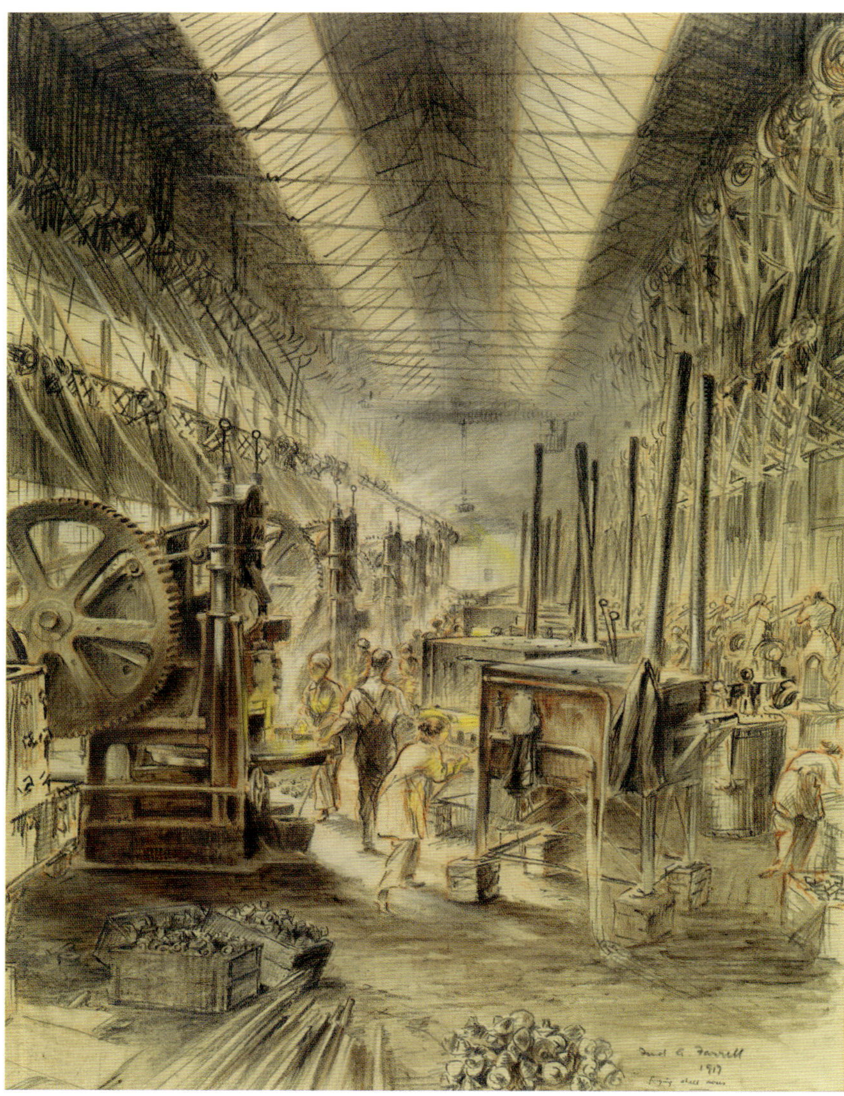

3

Forging Shell Noses

Signed and dated: 'Fred A. Farrell/1917'
Inscriptions: 'forging shell noses'; 'McL's'
Pencil, chalk and watercolour on paper
PR.1921.23.u

Farrell depicts the mechanical hammers
used to forge conical shell cases. The
machines are driven by overhead belts
linked to power shafts visible at the
top of the picture. These were usually
run by an engine positioned outside
the building. Boxes of shell noses can
be seen in the foreground waiting to be
heated in the central furnaces before
being forged in the machines to the
left and then cooled to the right of the
picture. Farrell uses a lively sketchiness
and a dynamic thrusting perspective
to convey the speed and energy of the
factory with its whirring belts, wheels
and shafts.

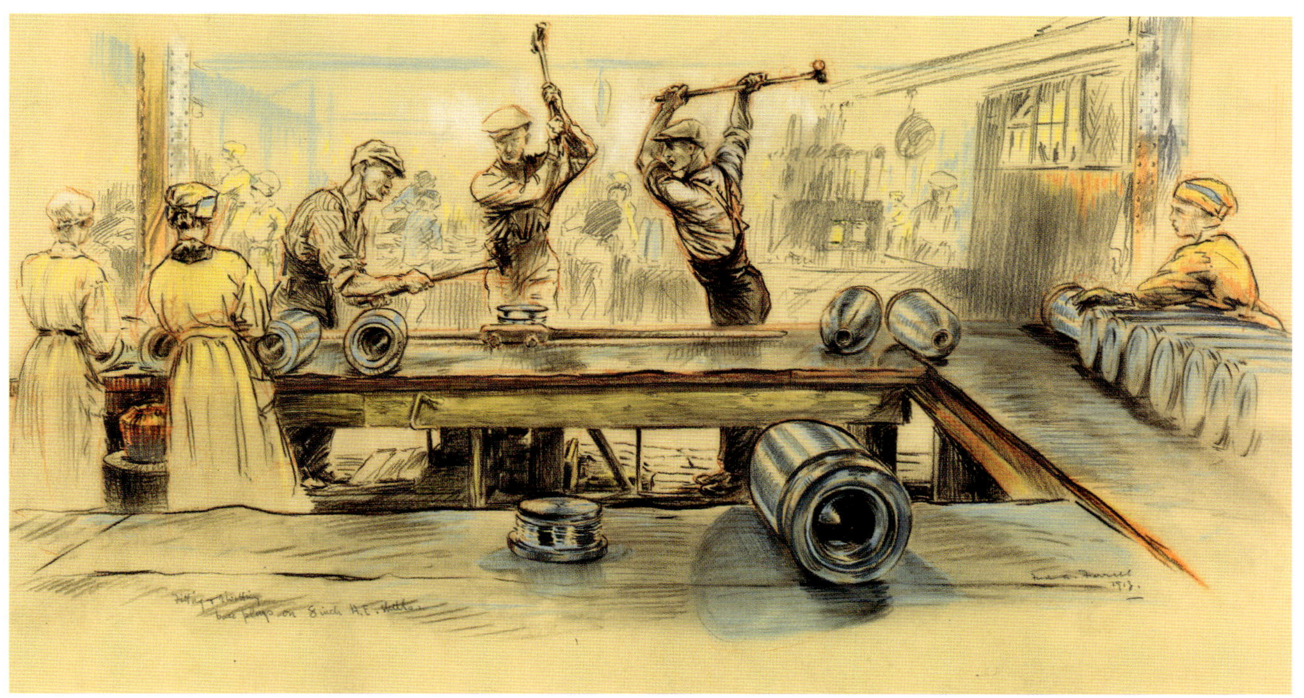

4

Fitting and Rivetting Base Plugs on 8-inch H.E. Shells

Signed and dated: 'Fred A. Farrell/1918'
Inscription: 'Fitting & rivetting base plugs on 8 inch H.E. shells'
Pencil and chalk on paper
PR.1921.23.v

This shows an efficient production line where the women roll the shells to and from the men who hammer the rivets. The men are noticeably older, younger men having been conscripted to Front Line service. Despite their age, Farrell patriotically shows the men carrying out heavy manual labour with energy, accuracy and rhythm.

He adds lively notes of yellow and blue to suggest a cheerful industriousness. The location may be the Cardonald Projectile Factory which from 1918 made 6-inch chemical shells as well as 8-inch high explosive shells.

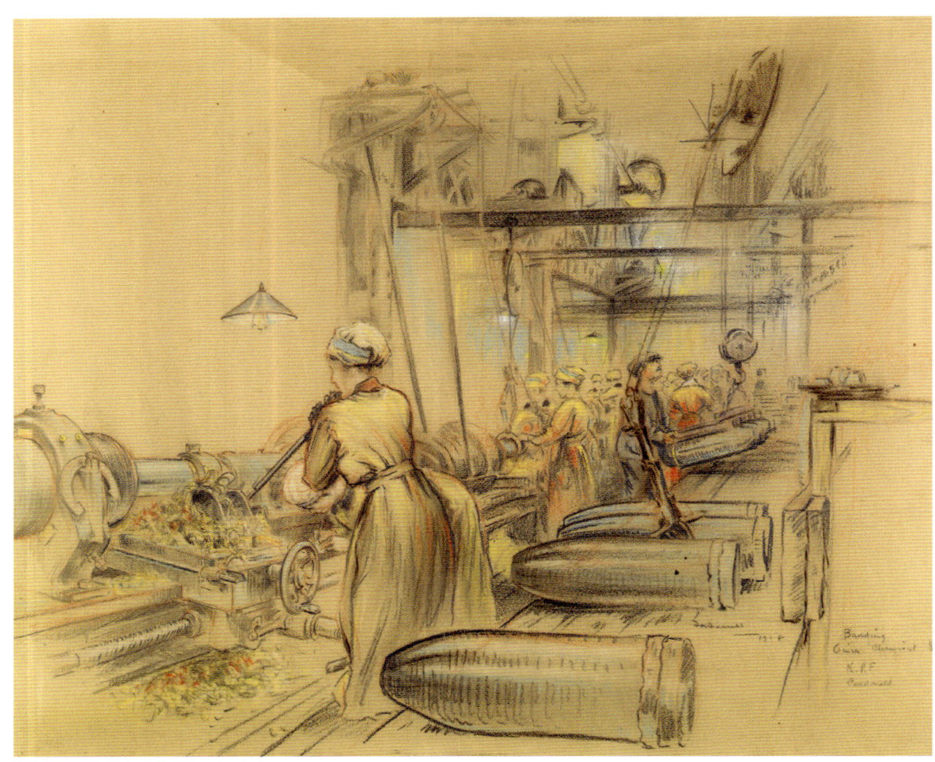

5

Banding 6-inch Chemical Shells, Cardonald

Signed and dated: 'F A Farrell 1918'
Inscription: 'Banding 6 inch Chemical
Shells N.P.F. Cardonald'
Pencil and chalk on paper
PR.1921.23.w

In this composition, Farrell draws on images of women in the traditional female role of the laundress. However, here the women are doing tasks formerly classed as men's work, using shaft-driven milling machines to prepare empty shell cases. The woman closest to the viewer, putting her back into the process, gives a sense of the physical effort involved.

Six-inch shells were a standard calibre in WWI for naval guns placed on a land carriage. A copper band was fitted in a groove around the shell to achieve a better seal and to impart a spin, giving improved range and accuracy. Chemical weapons were used extensively in WWI by both sides.

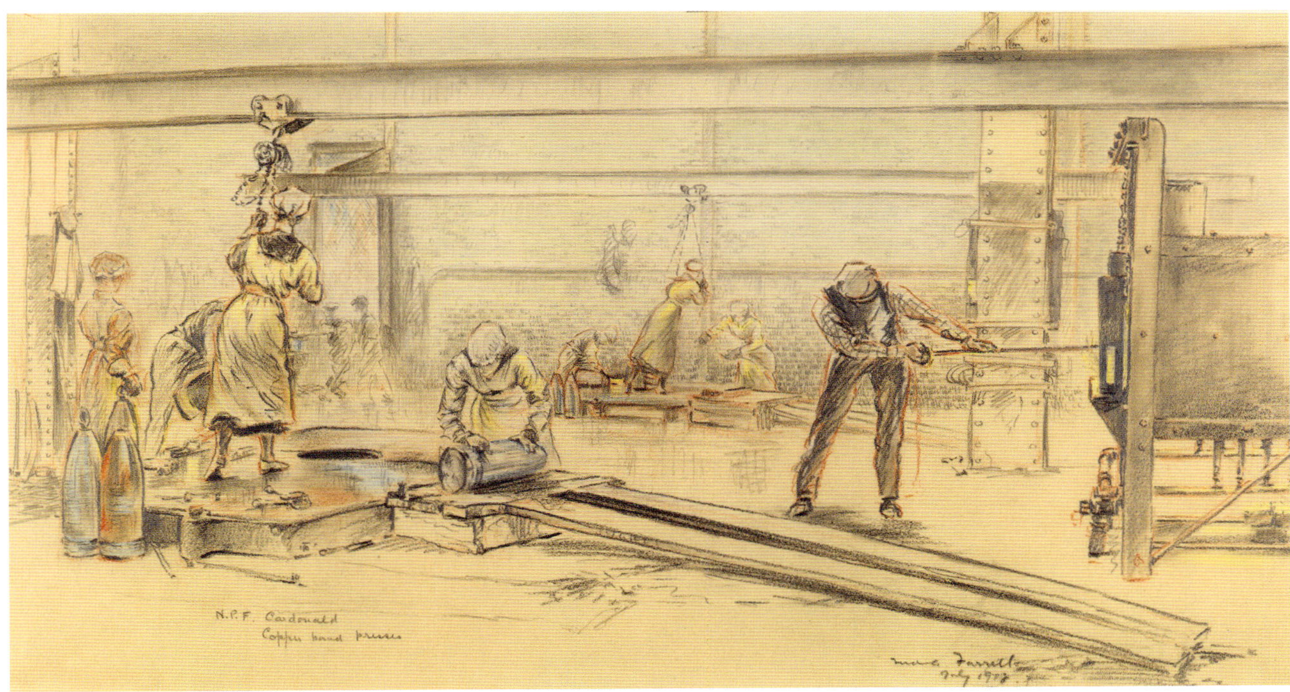

6
Copper Band Presses, Cardonald

Signed and dated: 'Fred A. Farrell/
July 1918'
Inscription: 'N.P.F. Cardonald/
Copper band presses'
Pencil and chalk on paper
PR.1921.23.z

Here empty shell cases are being
brought via overhead rails and rolled
on planks to furnaces where heated
copper bands are pressed into place.
Touches of yellow suggest the reflected
light and heat from the ovens. There is
a real sense of movement in the swish
of the women's skirts as they turn to
receive shells.

Men and women work together in
teams, apparently unaware of the artist's
eye. Farrell's drawings of the munitions
factories have the immediacy of on-the-
spot studies, in contrast to some of his
drawings of the Front Line which are
more obviously staged reconstructions.

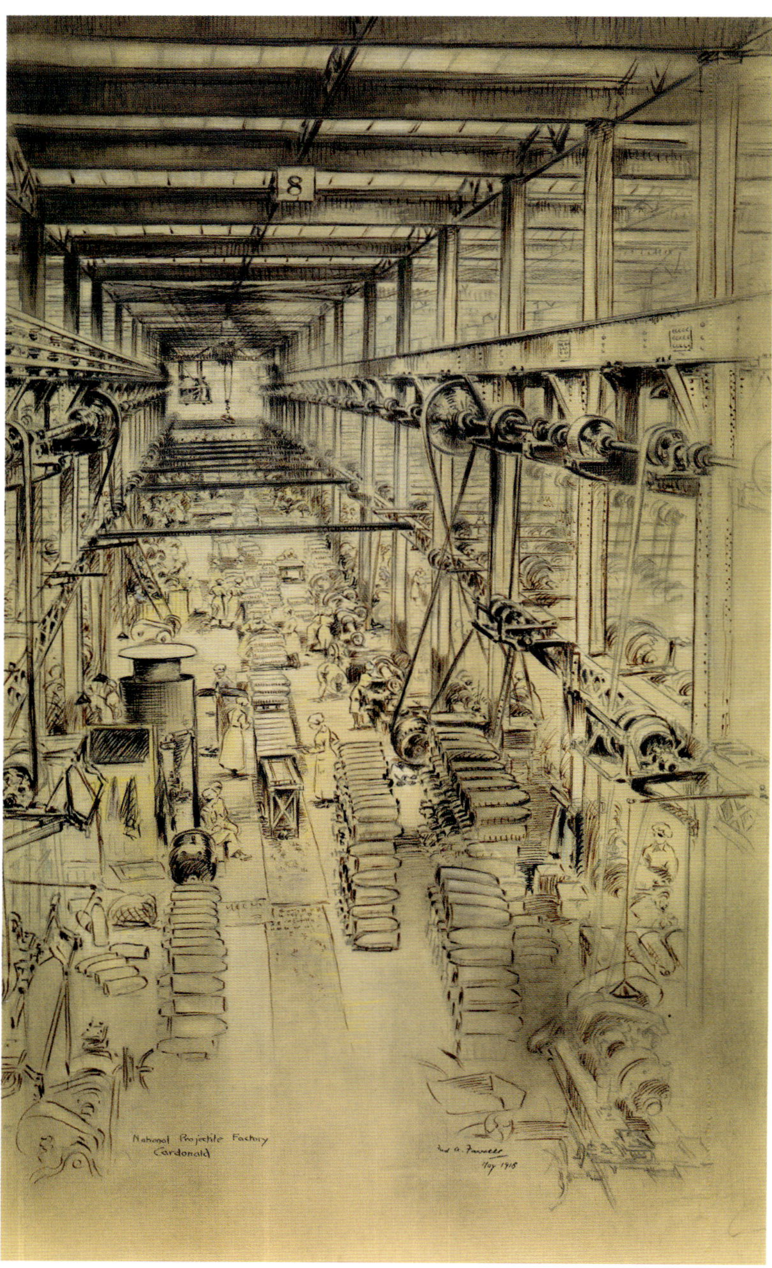

7
National Projectile Factory, Cardonald

Signed and dated, 'Fred A. Farrell/
May 1918'
Inscription: 'National Projectile Factory/
Cardonald'
Pencil and chalk on paper
PR.1921.23.ab

This drawing, which shows Farrell's
interest in structure, patterning and
design, focuses in a very modernist
way on the architecture of roof struts,
cast iron supports, power shafts and
driving belts. There is a feeling of
movement, energy and noise. The choice
of viewpoint emphasizes the height of
the factory and presents the production
hall as nave-like, the factory as the
new cathedral. The high vantage point
focuses on production in a broad sense
and distances the viewer from the reality
of the small figures of women using
machines to finish off shells.

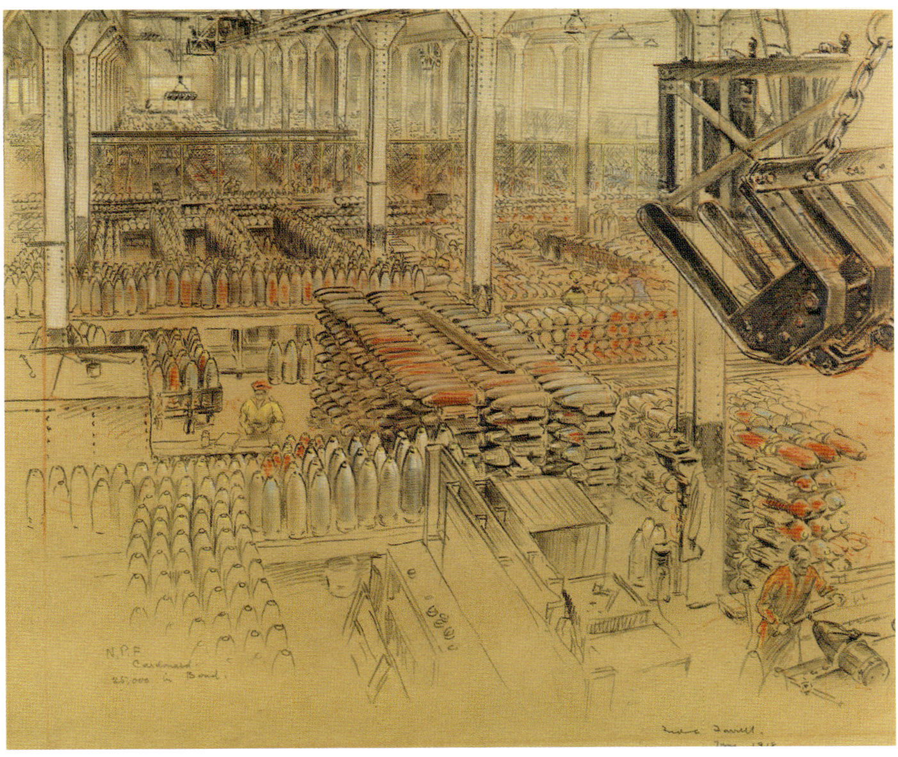

8

National Projectile Factory, Cardonald

Signed and dated, 'Fred A. Farrell/
June 1918'
Inscriptions: 'N.P.F. Cardonald/25,000
in Bond'; 'National Projectile Factory/
Cardonald'
Pencil and chalk on paper
PR.1921.23.aa

There is a sublime quality to this image of vast numbers of shells lined up and stacked in a huge factory hall. Farrell adopts a high viewpoint again, in order to give a sense of scale. The shells were counted in large batches of tens of thousands and approved by government inspectors before being shipped off by rail for use on the Front Line in France and Belgium.

They were picked up using the pronged buckets seen above on overhead rails. On the ground, workers make final checks. The whole, seen with an artist's eye, has a decorative, almost abstract, quality.

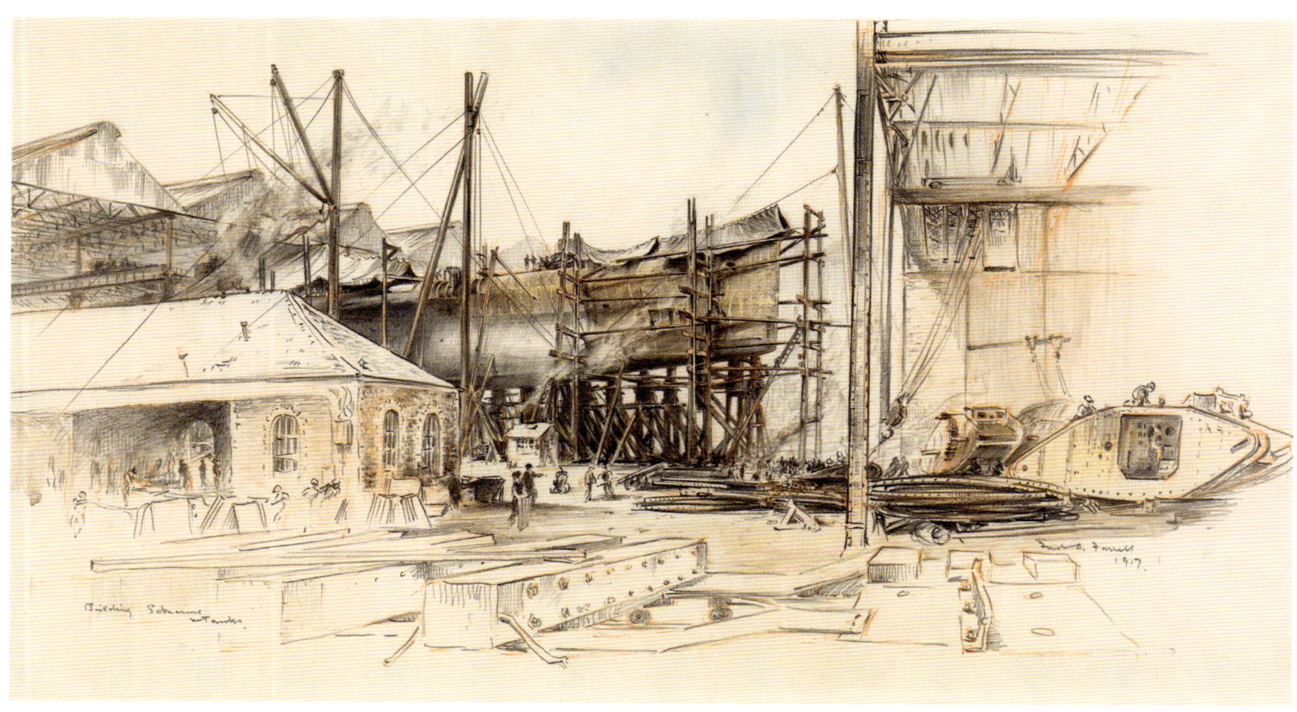

9
Building Submarines and Tanks

Signed and dated: 'Fred A. Farrell 1917'
Inscription: 'Building Submarine
and Tanks'
Pencil and chalk on paper
PR.1921.23.y

This may be John Brown's shipyard or Beardmore's Naval Construction Works, both of which were in Clydebank and built tanks and submarines. Farrell captures the scene from a slight distance in order to summarize the breadth of activity in the yard. Figures are left small and cipher-like. The artist's attention seems to be particularly drawn to the patterning created by the system of scaffolding, cranes and pulleys around the submarine, which, along with the support posts of the construction sheds and the iron girders lying prone in the foreground, give the picture definition and structure. This reminds us that Farrell's background was in civil engineering.

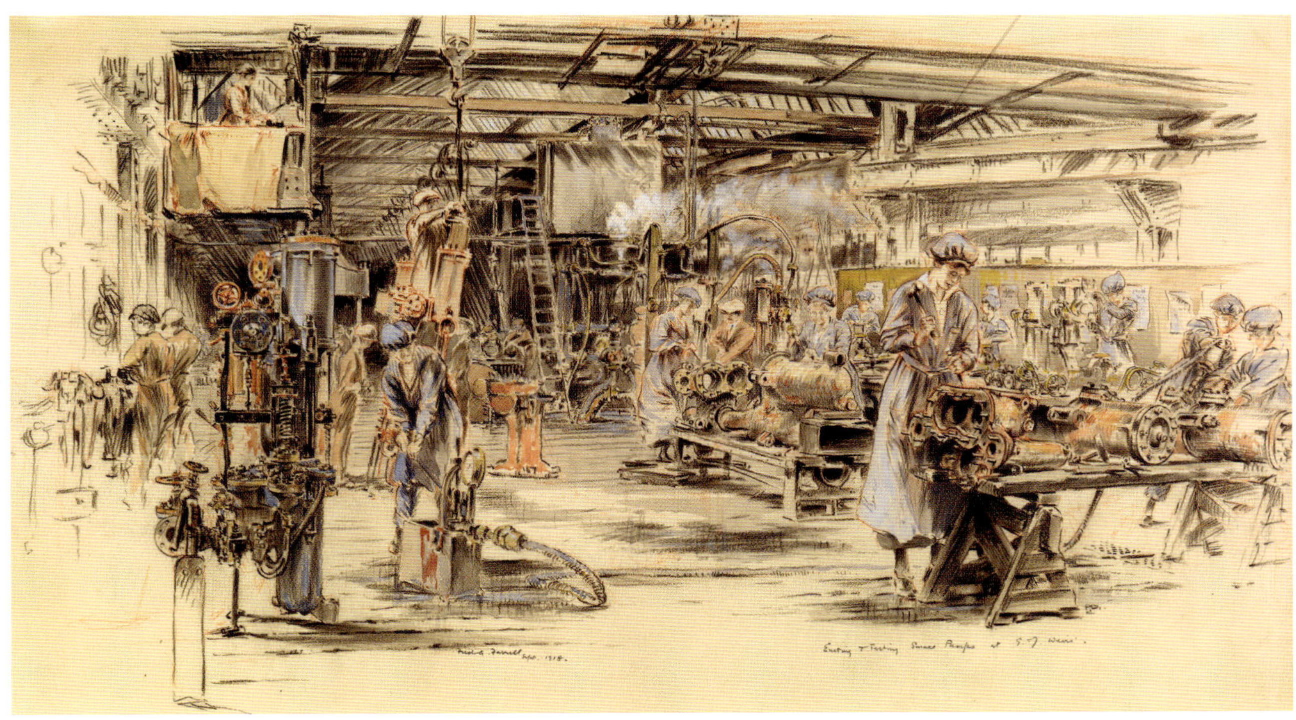

10
Erecting and Testing Small Pumps at G. & J. Weir

Signed and dated: 'Fred A. Farrell/
Sept. 1918'
Inscription: 'Erecting and Testing
Small Pumps at G. & J. Weirs'
Watercolour and chalk on paper
PR.1921.23.as

The women in this picture are hard at work making pumps at the engineering firm G. & J. Weir in Cathcart. Pumps such as these were used to keep trenches and dugouts on the Front Line free of water. The factory was also a major munitions and military aircraft supplier in WWI. The managing director, William Weir (1877–1959), later Viscount Weir of Eastwood, played a leading role in the Ministry of Munitions. This crowded drawing gives a sense of busy activity and productivity. It was exactly the kind of image that Glasgow wanted to project of itself, emphasizing the invaluable nature of its home contribution to the national war effort.

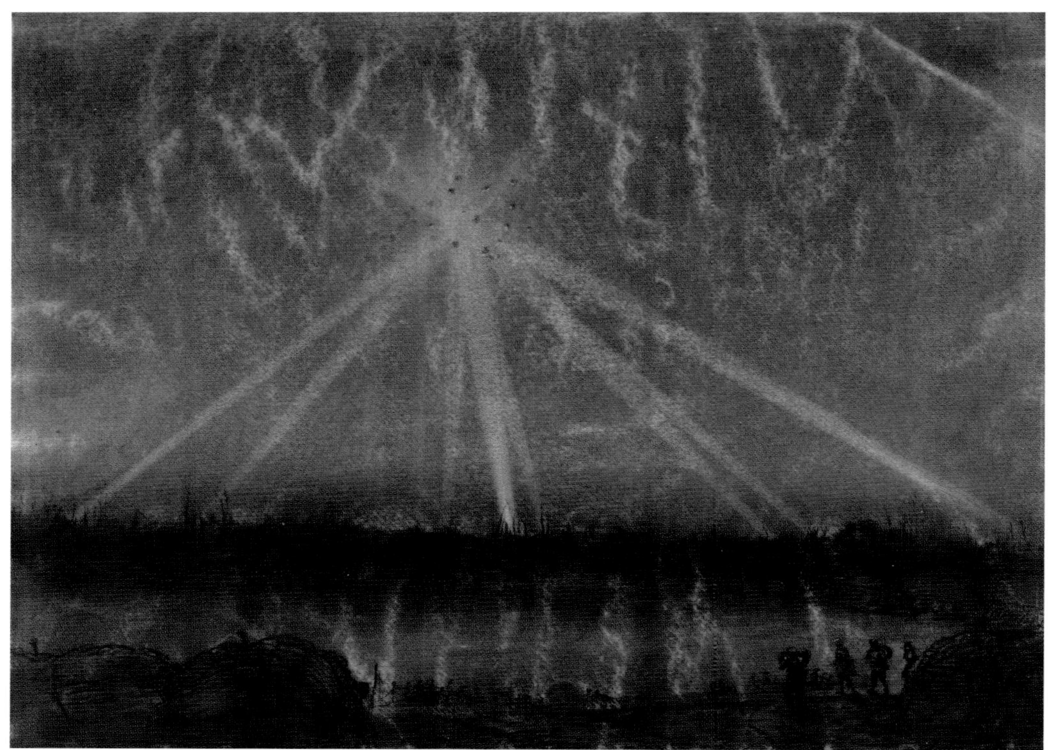

11

Searchlight Yser Canal

Unsigned
Ink, chalk and watercolour on paper
PR.1921.23.q

The Yser Canal, located just outside
Ypres in Flanders, was a major
obstacle for the German advance.
It was the scene of the Battle of Yser
in October 1914, and Farrell shows a
landscape marred by blighted trees,
sandbag defences and barbed wire
entanglements. He dramatically
depicts a German plane under anti-
aircraft fire as it is picked out by
defensive searchlights.

In this scene of strange beauty,
Farrell still retains a sense of humanity,
the viewer's eye being drawn to the
squad of soldiers bearing heavy sacks
in the foreground.

12

Battle Planes Attacking Bosche Scouting Planes with the Aid of Shrapnel Curtain Fire

Signed and dated: 'Fred A. Farrell/ Dec. 1917'
Inscription: 'Battle planes attacking Bosche scouting planes with aid of shrapnel curtain fire'
Chalk and watercolour on paper
PR.1921.23.r

Aerial warfare began in earnest in WWI. With a sense of visual theatre, Farrell shows, against a pastel blue sky, an air battle with swooping planes and puffs of anti-aircraft fire. Aerial reconnaissance was vital for creating plans of enemy defences, while intercepting enemy spotter planes was an important task in the intelligence war. The ground, which takes up only a fifth of the composition, is broken and marred by stumps of destroyed trees. Duckboards cross the wet, cratered ground and a row of crosses poignantly stands near a tangle of barbed wire.

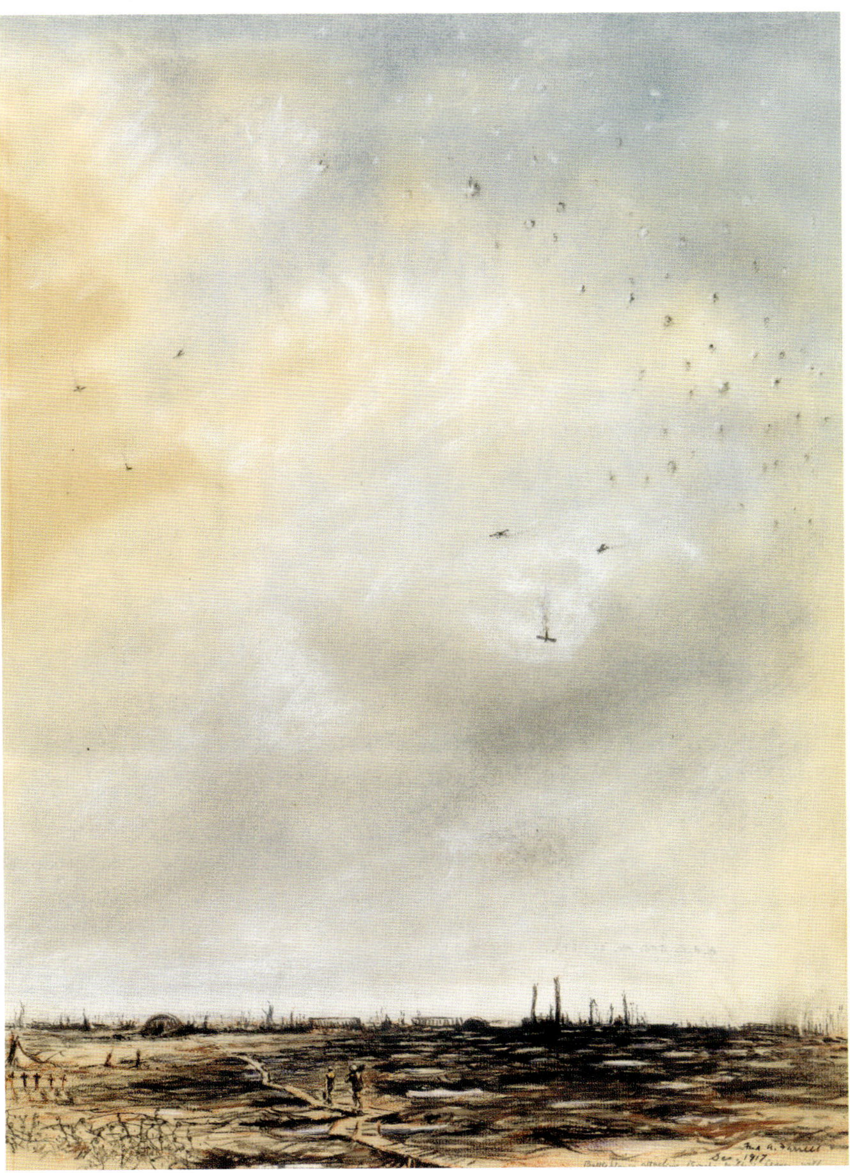

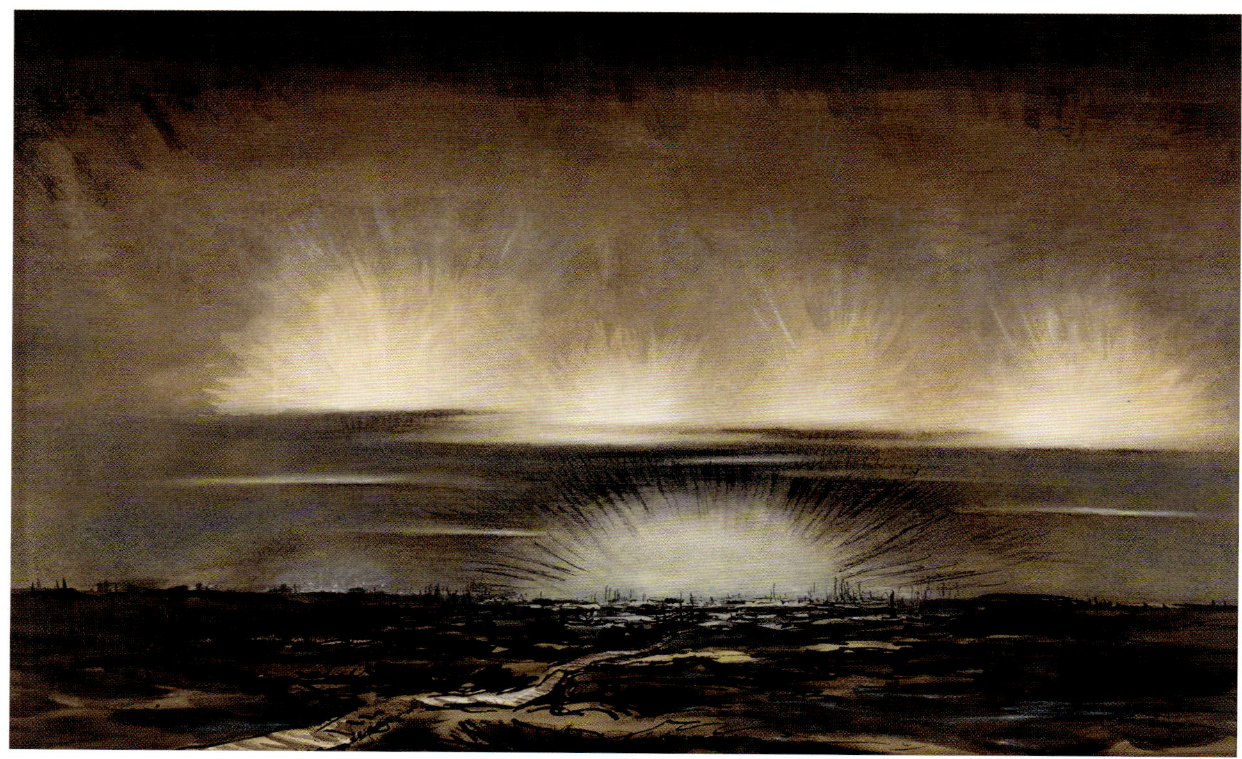

13

Ypres Salient – Drumfire 'Flashes'

Unsigned
Watercolour, ink and chalk on paper
PR.1921.23.ao

Drumfire was the name of a pattern of rapid artillery shellfire. It formed a deluge of explosive shells, making a barrier around a section of enemy territory before an attack. The impact of this on the landscape can be seen in the foreground with shell craters that could only be crossed using wooden pathways.

The bright explosions are reflected off low clouds, transforming this terrifying scene into something of sublime beauty.

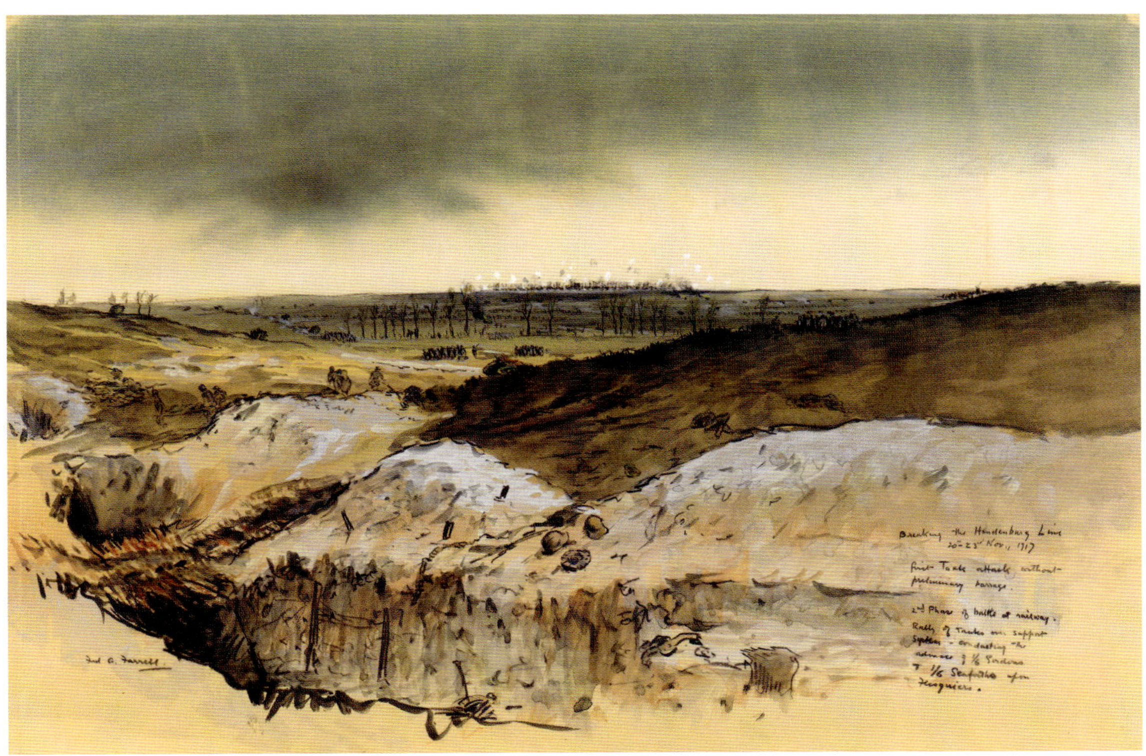

14

Breaking the Hindenburg Line

Signed: 'Fred A. Farrell'
Inscription: 'Breaking the Hindenburg
Line/20th–23rd Nov., 1917/first Tank
attack without preliminary barrage./
2nd Phase of battle at railway./Rally of
Tanks over support system – conducting
the advance of 1/6 Gordons and 1/6
Seaforths upon Flesquieres'
Chalk and watercolour on paper
PR.1921.23.0

The Hindenburg Line was a system
of strong defences built by the German
army in 1916–17. They were attacked
during the Battle of Cambrai in
November and December 1917. One
of the strongest points was Flesquières,
seen here on the skyline, which was
attacked by the 51st (Highland)
Division. In this panoramic drawing,
Farrell shows the white puffs of an
artillery shell attack, with lines of
soldiers following tanks into attack.
This was the first use of tanks in large
numbers. In the foreground, troops and
stretcher bearers clear casualties from
the German support trenches. Farrell
uses fallen helmets to represent the
casualties that government censorship
prevents him from portraying.

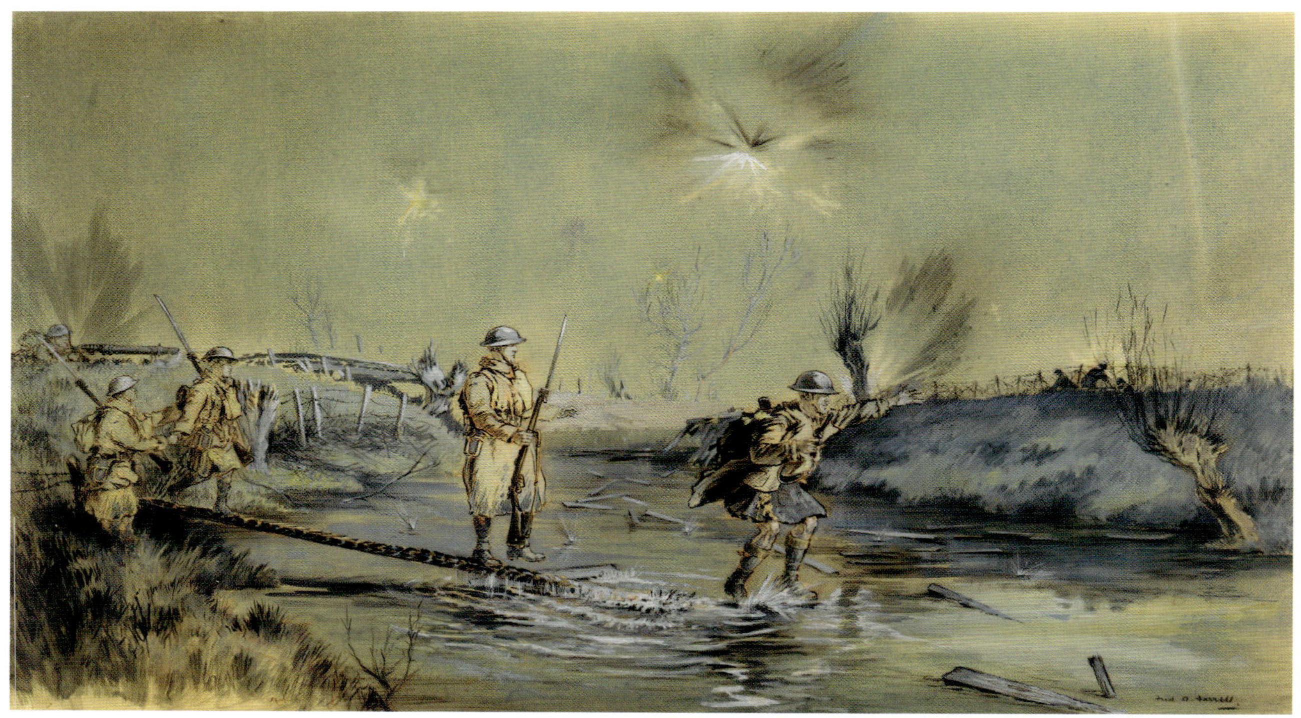

15
Crossing of the Ecaillon

Signed: 'Fred A. Farrell'
Inscription: 'Crossing the Ecaillon'
Pencil and watercolour on paper
PR.1921.23.a

On 24 October 1918 in one of the last assaults of the war, the 51st (Highland) Division experienced difficulties crossing the River Ecaillon at the village of Monchaux. This picture shows Lieutenant Walker of the 6th Black Watch (Royal Highlanders) heroically leading his platoon, having made the decision to abandon troublesome duckboards and cross the icy river wearing their heavy greatcoats and backpacks. Farrell enhances the drama, depicting shells exploding and the enemy setting barbed wire on the far side. He uses the two men on the left who are helping each other to project a sense of solidarity under strain.

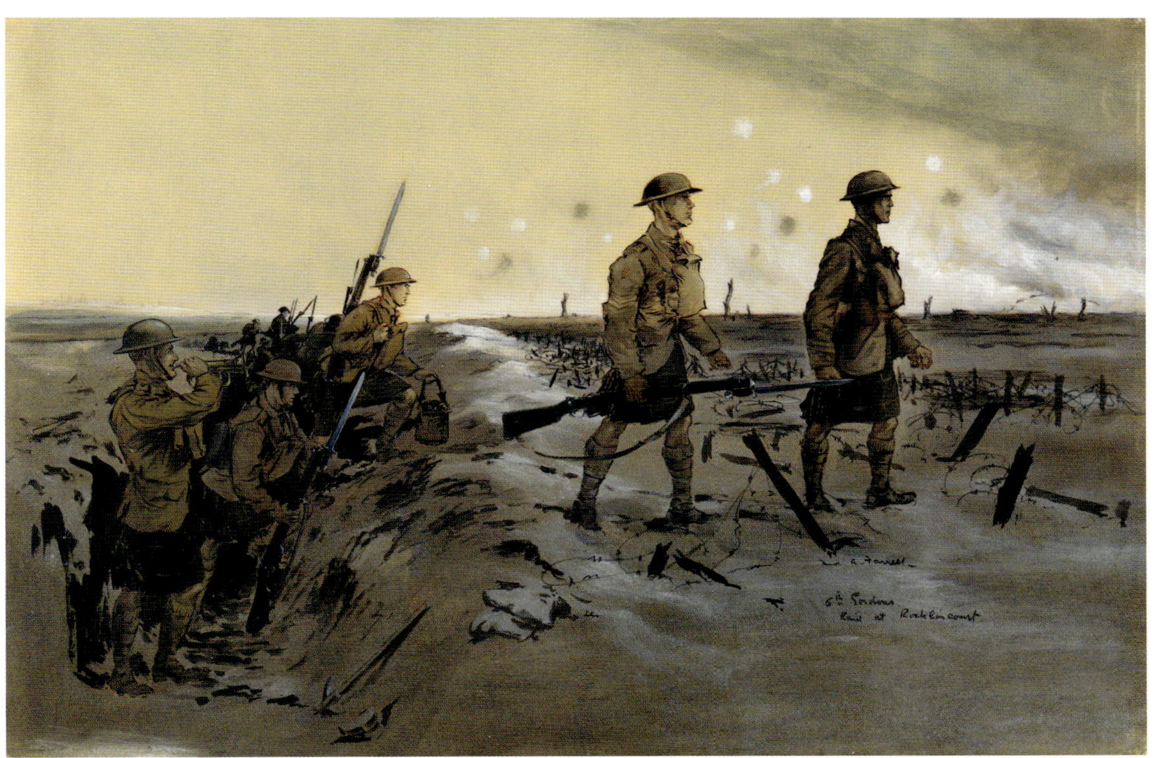

16
Daylight Raid by the 6th Gordons at Roclincourt

Signed: 'Fred A. Farrell'
Inscription: '6th Gordons./
Raid at Rocklincourt'
Chalk, pencil and watercolour
on paper
PR.1921.23.m

Lieutenant Clark and his men are shown stoically setting off on a raid in early light over snow-covered ground through barbed wire. Vimy Ridge, the scene of awful fighting, can be seen in the background. It was captured by Canadians in early 1917. Raids were encouraged in order to unsettle the enemy and to capture prisoners who were then interrogated for information.

These men are not wearing their full equipment and heavy packs so that they can move swiftly and silently. Their coats have a distinctive cut at the front to allow a sporran to be worn.

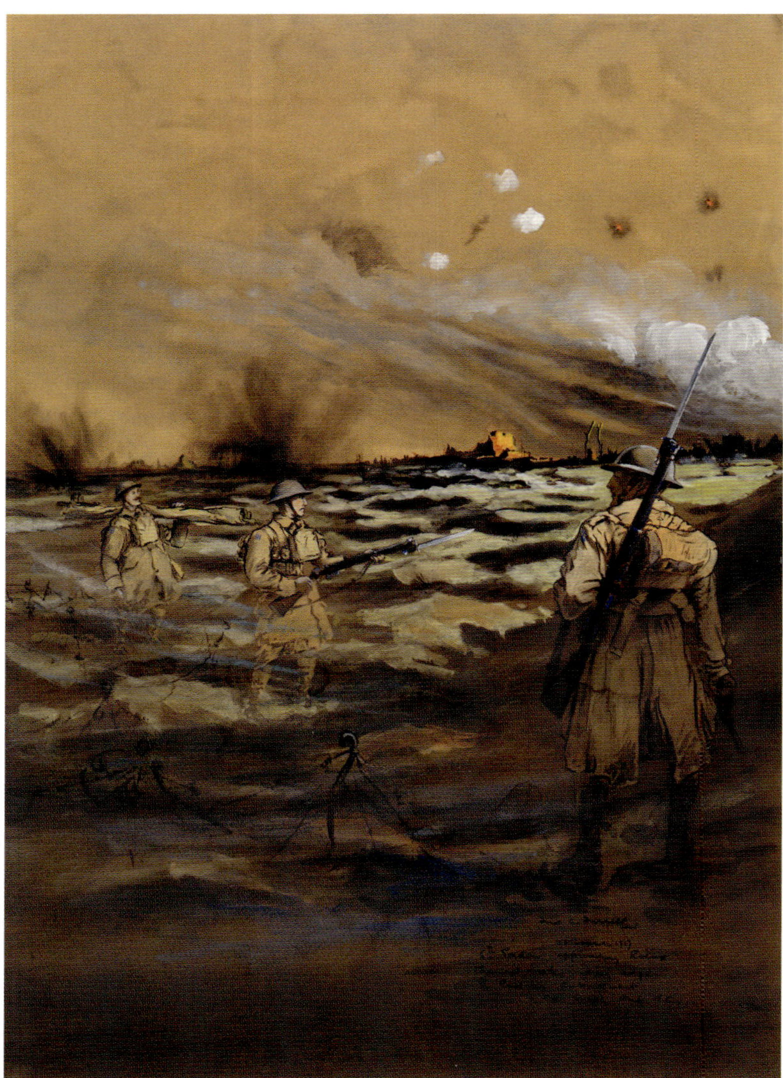

17
6th Gordons at Roeux Chemical Works

Signed and dated: 'Fred A. Farrell'
Inscription: '23 April 1917/6th Gordons approaching Roeux Chemical works along edge of Railway embankment./ Capt. Ralph Risk, M.C.'
Chalk and watercolour on paper
PR.1921.23.i

On 23 April 1917, Highlanders of the 51st Division attacked the chemical works at Roeux just outside Arras, France. Farrell theatrically highlights the factory buildings castle-like on the horizon, bathed in a golden light. The attack was met with machine gun fire from Greenland Hill. A railway embankment just out of the picture shelters these men from the bullets. However, there were very heavy casualties, to which the dramatically pitted landscape and stretcher bearer on the left allude.

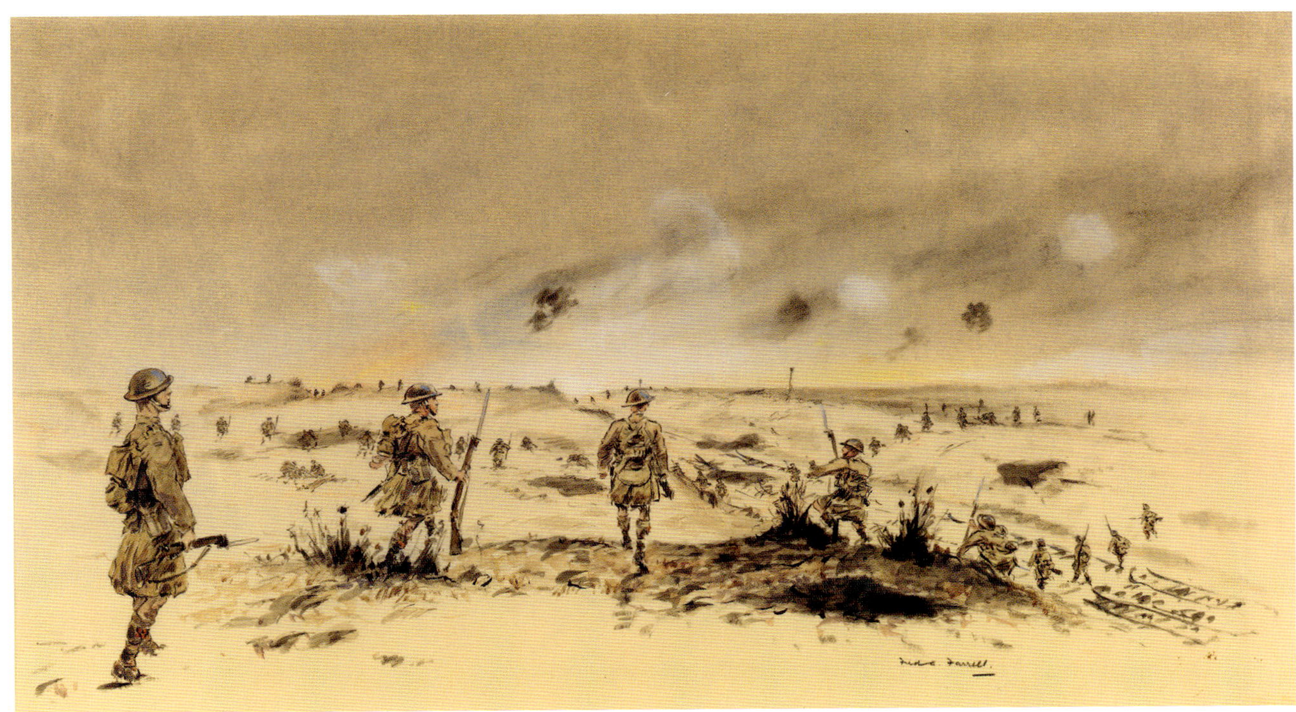

18

4th Gordons Clearing the Crest of Greenland Hill and 'Windmill Copse'

Signed: 'Fred A. Farrell'
Inscription: '4th Gordons clearing out of Greenland Hill at Windmill Copse'
Chalk and watercolour on paper
PR.1921.23.n

Rows of kilted Highlanders can be seen moving forward to capture Greenland Hill, an area of strategic significance to the north east of Arras in France, during the Battle of the Scarpe in August 1918. By this time, infantry attacks were delivered in waves, the first of which would follow just behind a barrage of exploding shells and slip through gaps in enemy defences.

The second and third waves were often called 'worms', to describe their wriggly appearance from a distance. A fourth wave of men would defend any captured ground from counterattack.

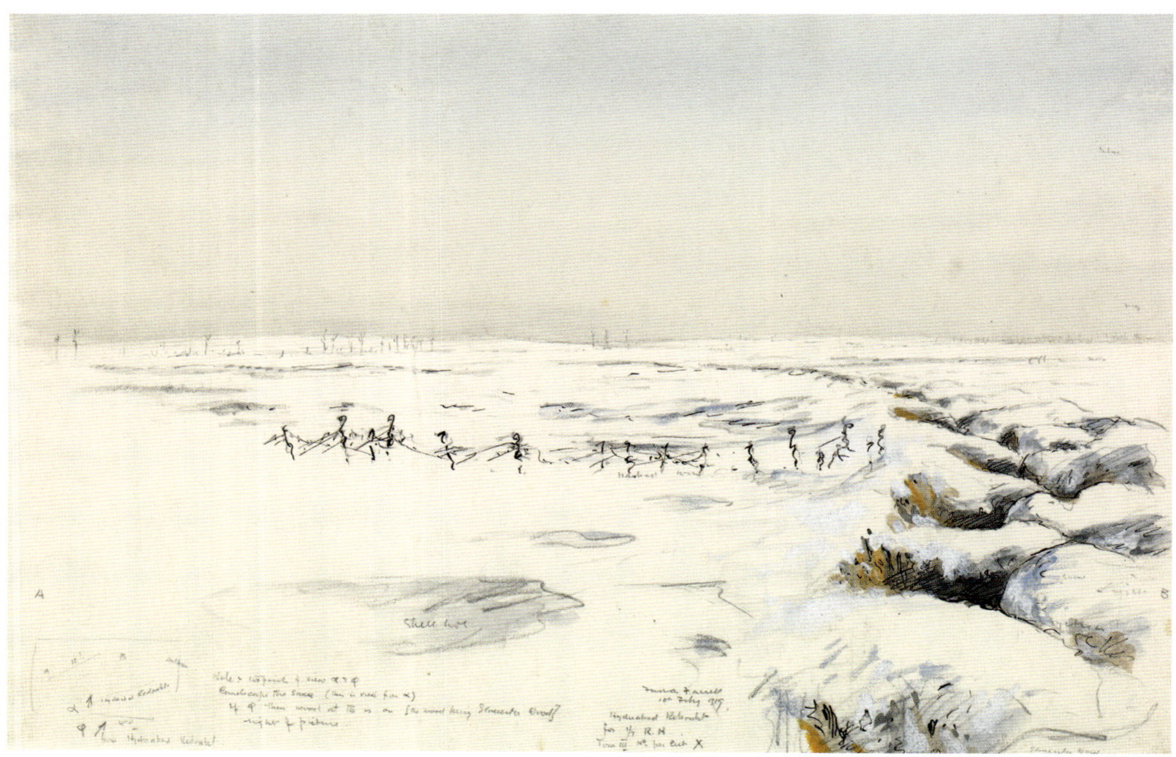

19
The Hyderabad Redoubt

Signed and dated: 'Fred A. Farrell/
18th July 1919'
Inscriptions: 'Hyderabad Redoubt/for
1/7 R.H./Tom III No per cut X'; 'Note:
two points of view ⤬ & φ/landscape
the same (this is view from ⤬)/If φ
then wood at B is on [the wood being
Gloucester Wood] right of picture.';
[small diagram] '/Hyderabad Redoubt _
from Hyderabad Redoubt'; 'blue'; 'grey';
'greyish'; 'brown'; 'barbed wire'; 'Shell
hole'; 'snow'; 'yellow'; 'light'

Pencil, ink, watercolour and
bodycolour on paper
PR.1921.23.b

German fortifications were strong and
well defended. The Hyderabad Redoubt
strongpoint protected the Arras to Lille
Road, shown by the trees at the top of
the picture. In the distance on the right
can be seen Gloucester Wood. The 51st
(Highland) Division experienced terrible
fighting here before the strongpoint

was taken. The landscape was left
devastated, full of shell holes, ruined
trenches and barbed wire. Farrell made
extensive notes to himself regarding
aspects of the landscape and the
colours to apply when he worked his
pencil sketch up into a more finished
work back home. There is a small
interpretative sketch at the bottom left.

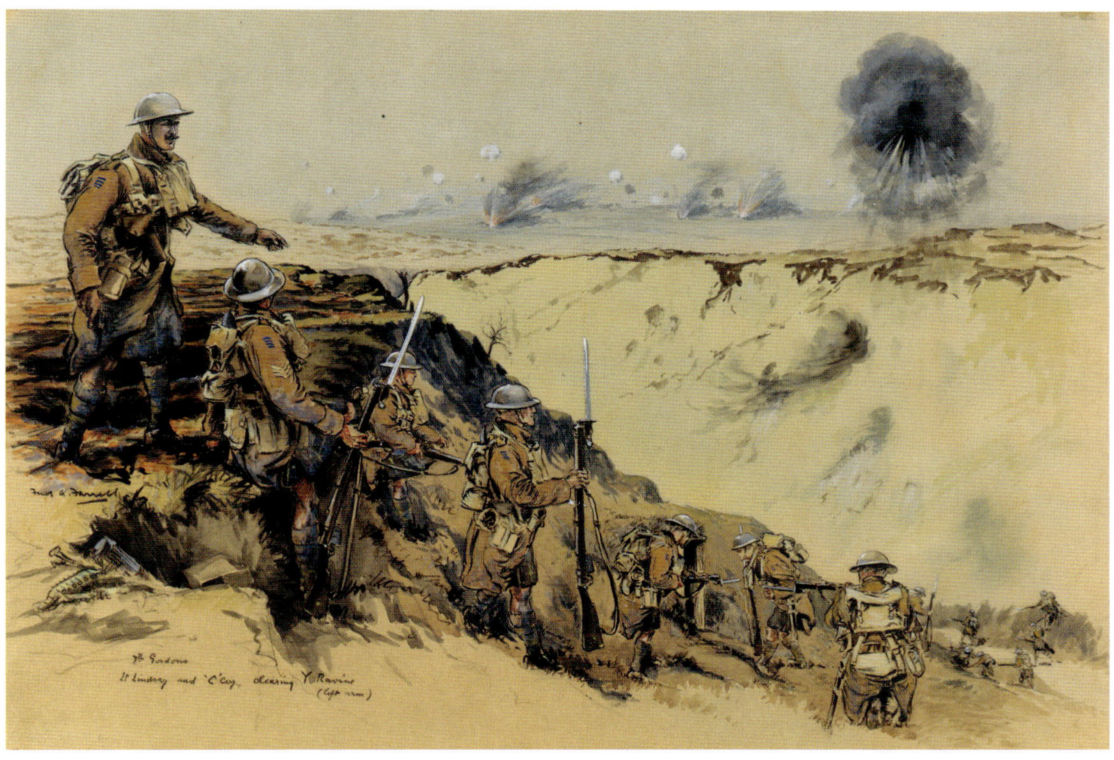

20

7th Gordons Clearing 'Y' Ravine

Signed: 'Fred A. Farrell'
Inscription: '7th Gordons/Lt Lindsay
and 'C' Coy clearing Y Ravine (left arm)'
Chalk and watercolour on paper
PR.1921.23.c

This drawing shows the advance
on Beaumont-Hamel from the
Auchonvillers region, which took place
on 13 November 1916. Farrell depicts
Lieutenant R.G. Lindsay, bravely
silhouetted above the horizon line,
leading 'C' Company, 7th Gordons, as
they use grenades to clear enemy troops
from deep underground bunkers dug
into the side of the ravine.

The Battle of the Ancre rages in the
background with shells bursting on
'Munich' Trench. The gesture of Lindsay,
and the line of rocks which lead our eye
into the ravine, remind the viewer that
this is an artistic reconstruction.

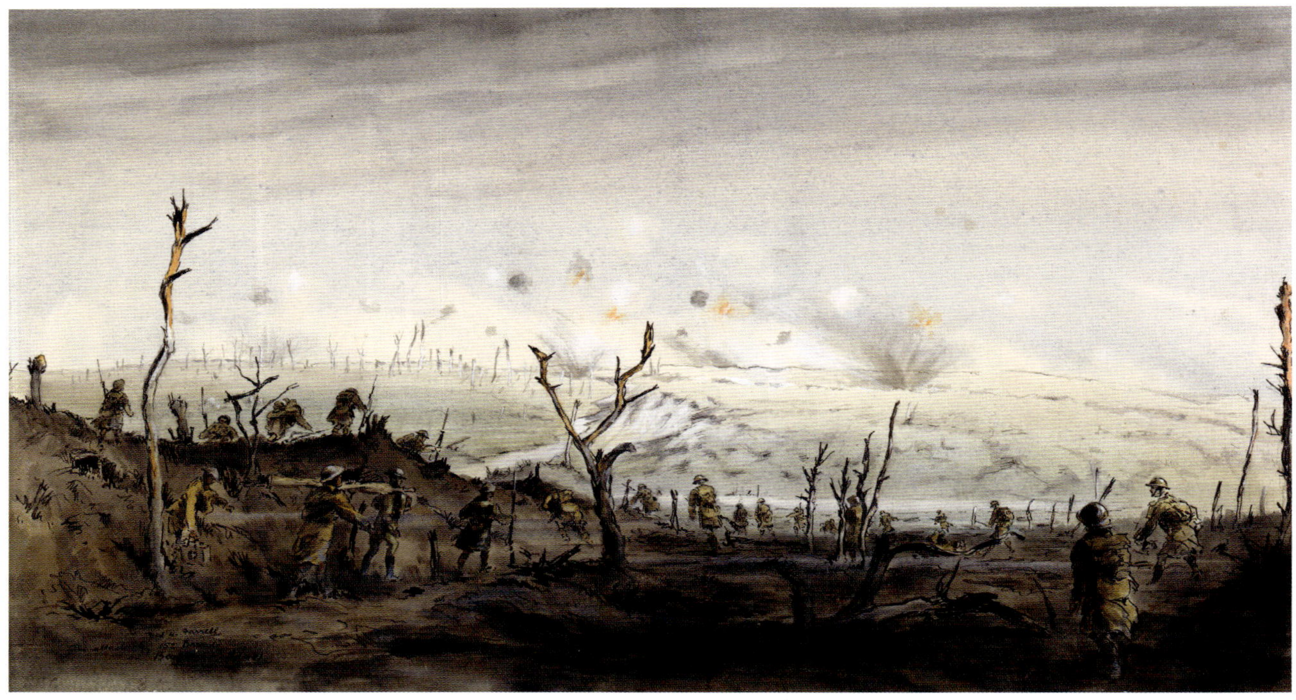

21

Beaumont-Hamel

Signed: 'Fred A. Farrell'
Inscription: 'The attack by 152 Brigade on Beaumont Hamel'
Ink, watercolour and bodycolour on paper
PR.1921.23.k

On 13 November 1916, after 'Y' Ravine was taken, the Highlanders attacked Beaumont-Hamel. Beyond a disused quarry in the middle ground, shells explode on 'Munich' Trench. Rows of soldiers advance into enemy gunfire, trying to keep up with their own barrage of shells being fired just ahead of them.

The ravaged landscape is punctured by the broken silhouettes of trees shredded by flying metal from shells. Censorship meant that war artists could not show dead bodies, but the doctor and stretcher bearer at the left are poignant reminders of the horrors of war.

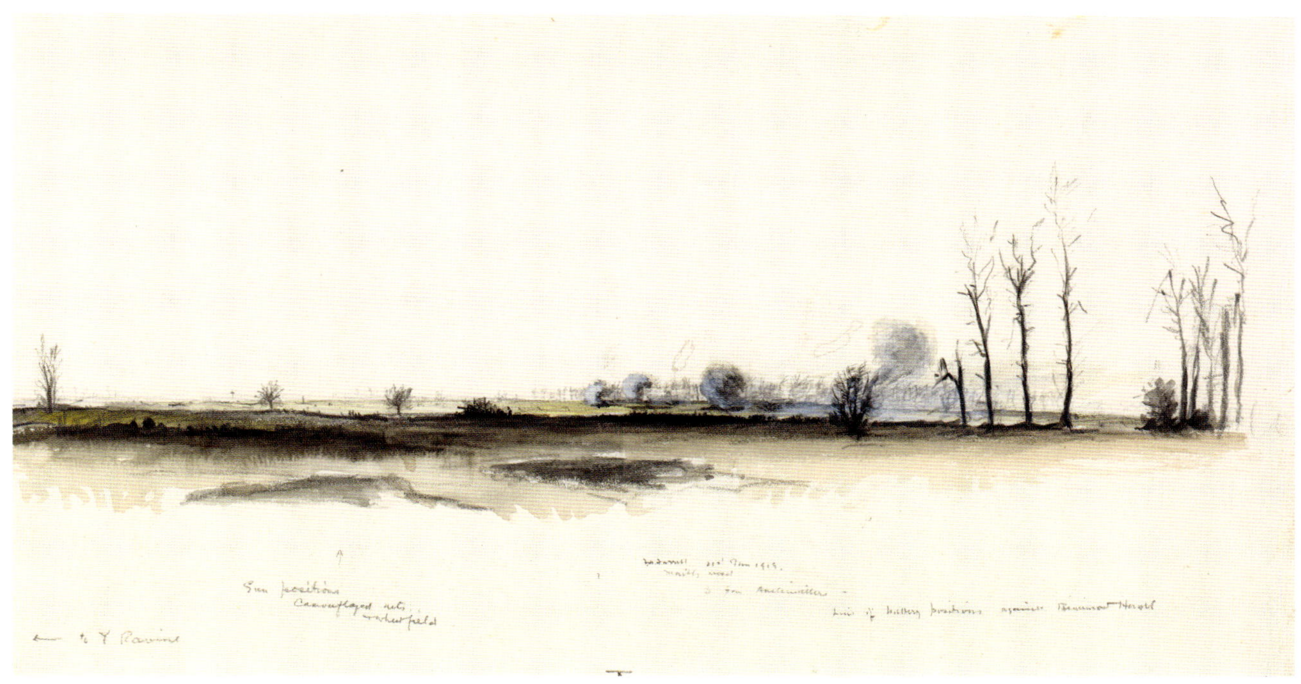

22

Battery Positions between Auchonvillers and Maillet-Mailly Wood

Signed and dated: 'F. A. Farrell
21st Jan 1919.'
Inscriptions: 'Battery positions between
Auchonvillers and Maillet-Mailly Wood/
from Auchonvillers'; 'View of battery
positions against Beaumont Hamel';
'← to Y Ravine'; '↑ Gun positions/
camouflaged nets./& wheatfield'; '↓
Auchonvillers'; 'Mailly Wood'; 'S from
Auchonvillers'; 'Line of battery positions
against Beaumont Hamell'

Pencil and watercolour on paper
PR.1921.23.d

Farrell's inscriptions point to the fact
that the rather bare foreground in
this delicate watercolour actually hides
guns in camouflaged pits. These were
used to support the 51st (Highland)
Division's attack on 'Y' Ravine and
Beaumont Hamel.

Farrell picks out small figures and
guns in ink on the rise. Explosions can
be seen in the field beyond. Farrell's
inscriptions highlight that this was
formerly productive farmland.

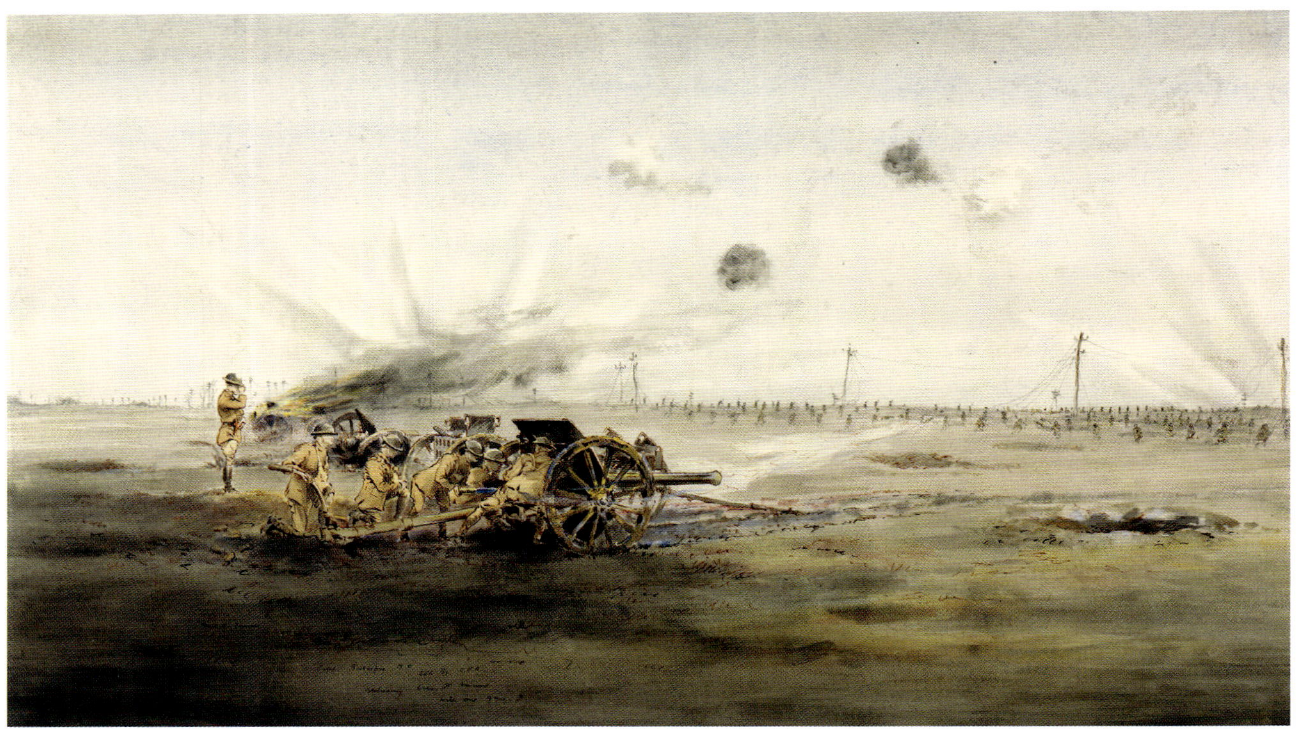

23

Lieutenant J. Gillespie, M.C., 256th Brigade, R.F.A., Before Lieu St Amand

Signed: 'Fred A. Farrell'
Inscription: 'Capt. Gillespie M.C. 256
Bg. R.F.A./reducing Lieu St Amand
with one gun.'
Ink and watercolour on paper
PR.1921.23.1

Highlanders attacking Avesnes-le-Sec on 13 October 1918 were devastated by machine gun fire from the village of Lieu-Saint-Amand. In the middle ground Farrell shows one of the guns of the 256th Royal Field Artillery being destroyed, while another returns fire. This early type of artillery was the most common in British service in Europe, although it was designed for an age before trench warfare, being ineffective at tasks such as breaking barbed wire. Equally anachronistic are the neat rows of men that can be seen advancing past the telegraph poles on the horizon. Farrell was a soldier in the early years of the war but by late 1918 this type of formation would not have been used.

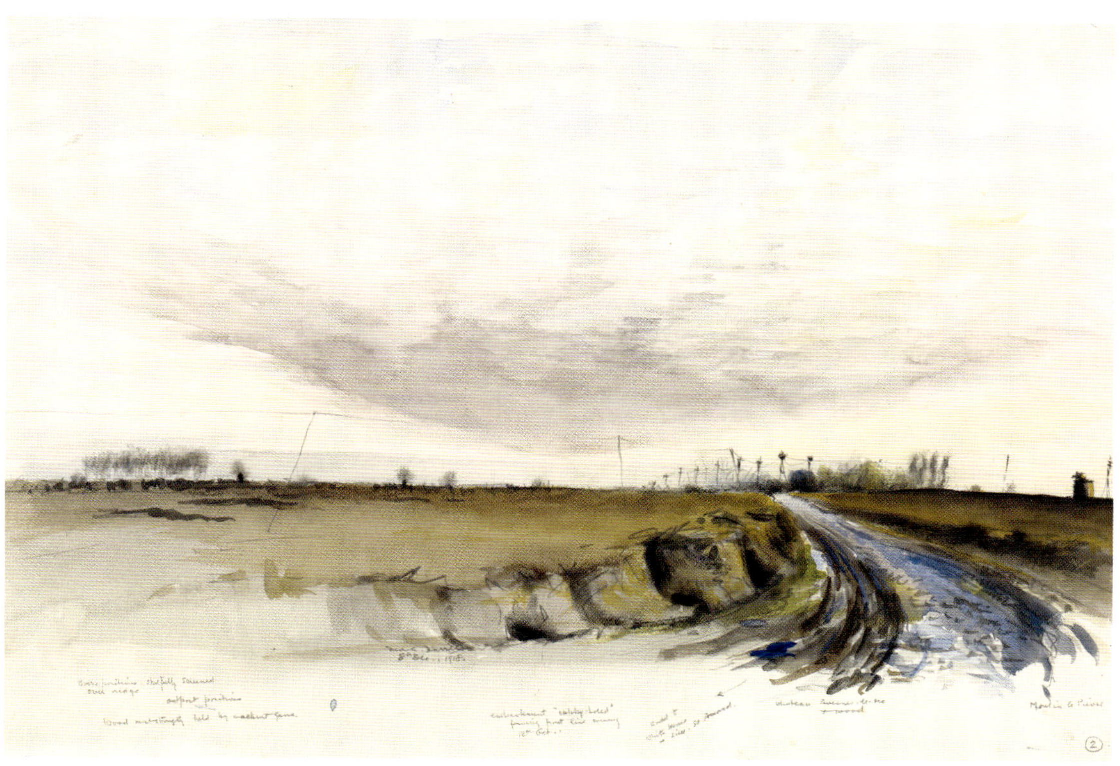

24

The 'Edge of the Upland' from Lieu St Amand Road

Signed and dated: 'Fred A. Farrell/
8th Dec., 1918.'
Inscriptions: 'Boche positions skillfully
secured/over ridge.'; 'outpost positions';
'Wood most strongly held by machine
guns.'; 'embankment "cubby-holed"/
forming front line evening/12th Oct.';
'Road to/White House & Lieu-St
Amand.'; 'Chateau Avesnes-le-sec &
wood'; 'Moulin le Pierre'; '2. [circled]'

Watercolour and pencil on paper
PR.1921.23.e

This deceptively still scene shows the
crest of a hill beyond which lay a wood
heavily defended by machine guns.
Safety holes can be seen dug into the
embankment at the side of the road.
The Gordon Highlanders suffered
considerable casualties crossing the

skyline. A windmill on the right has
been shorn of its sails. Although this is a
landscape of quiet menace, Farrell sees
something decorative in the blue of the
puddles after rainfall, beside the yellow-
green of the fields.

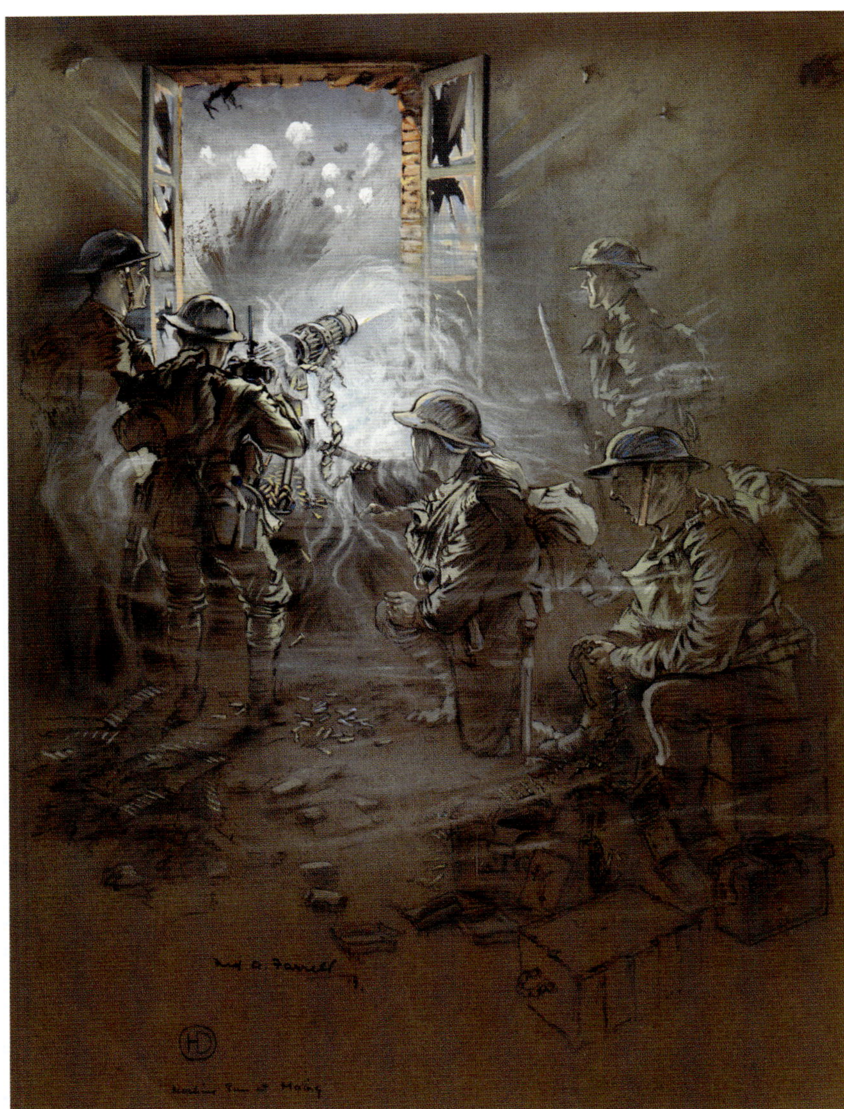

25

Machine Gun in House at Maing

Signed: 'Fred A. Farrell 19.'
Inscription: 'Machine Gun at Maing'
Chalk and watercolour on paper
PR.1921.23

Farrell shows Lieutenant Davies and his men using a heavy machine gun from an upstairs window to help their comrades' attack at Famars Ridge in October 1918. Most buildings at the Front Line had been flattened by artillery fire, so these men are very exposed. Exploding shells can be seen outside. This Vickers gun needed several men to operate it, feeding the belts of ammunition while others keep a lookout. Spent belts and cartridge cases litter the floor. If properly fed, with ammunition and water for cooling, this type of gun could fire for 12 hours nonstop. This drawing was probably one of those works completed in Farrell's London studio in the spring of 1919, after the war had ended.

26

'Surrender Englander!' – Neuville St Vaast

Signed: 'Fred A. Farrell'
Inscription: '"Surrender
Englander!"/8th Argyll incident'
Chalk, bodycolour and ink on dark
brown paper
PR.1921.23.j

This poster-like propagandist piece
is a reconstruction of a much recounted
event that reportedly took place in
April 1916. During darkness a German
officer climbed the barbed wire, pointed
his revolver into a British trench and
shouted, 'Surrender Englander!' An
NCO of the 8th Argyll & Sutherland
Highlanders, who was stationed in
the trench, had a hand grenade in
his hand. Without pulling the pin, he
threw it at the German, shouting, 'I am
no Englander; I'm a Scotsman!' The
force of the blow killed the German.
Apparently it was later discovered from
German prisoners that this incident
prevented a further attack.

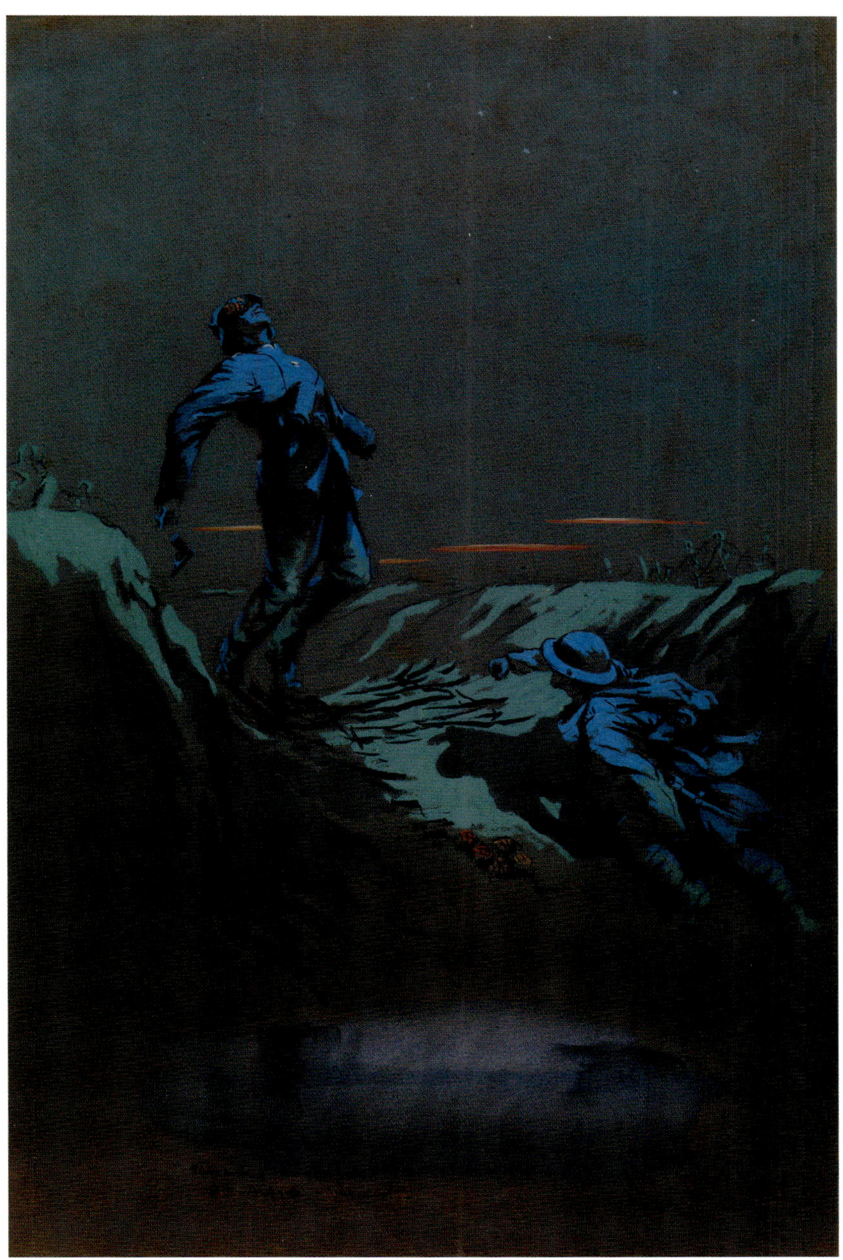

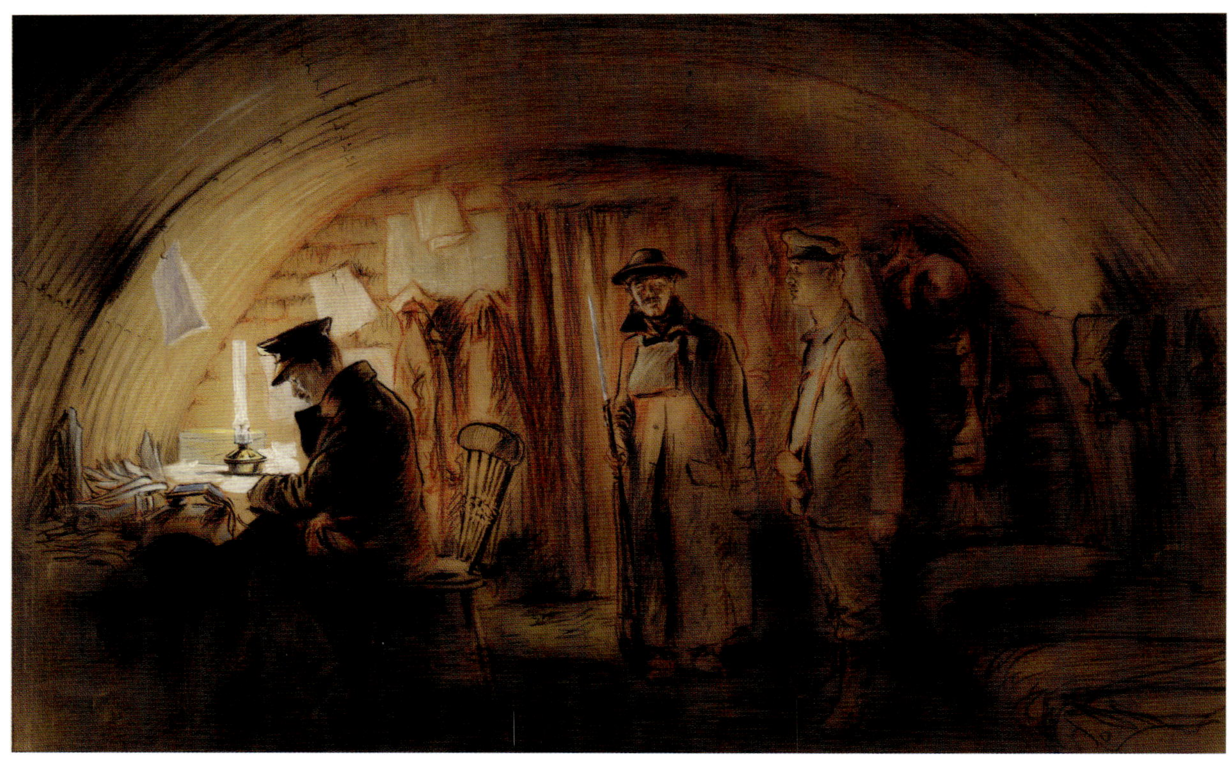

27

Intelligence Officer's Shelter. Prisoner Awaiting Re-examination

Inscription: 'Intelligence
Officers shelter/Prisoner awaiting
re-examination'
Crayon and chalk on paper
PR.1921.23.ae

A German prisoner wearing binoculars – possibly an artilleryman who spots targets for his guns – waits to be questioned. The underground bunker has an arched roof made of corrugated iron, or 'wriggly tin', which helps to spread the weight of the earth above it. A curtain is the only door to the officer's quarters, which serves as office and bedroom.

Farrell uses the light coming from the oil lamp to silhouette the thoughtful figure of the intelligence officer. War artists were made very aware of the importance in presenting the war as just; here there is no sense of violence or threat, but rather of cautious suspicion exuding from the guard holding his rifle and bayonet.

28

Corridor of Captured Pillbox,
Ypres

Signed: 'Fred A. Farrell'
Inscription: 'Corridor of captured
Pill-box 'Alberta'. Ypres Salient 1917.
H.L.I. officers reporting at
97th Brigade H.Qrs'
Pastel on paper
PR.1921.23.ar

This dimly lit corridor is an
underground view of the German
bunker 'Alberta', captured in 1917.
German bunkers were built with walls
of thick wood and reinforced concrete
and could be many metres beneath
the ground, offering a high degree of
protection from artillery fire. Farrell
populates the bunker with two officers
in trench coats and riding breeches;
the one on the left wears puttees over
his boots, the other wears riding boots.
Through the blue light and hunched
figures, Farrell conveys the realities of
trench life in winter. Socks can be seen
hanging up to dry.

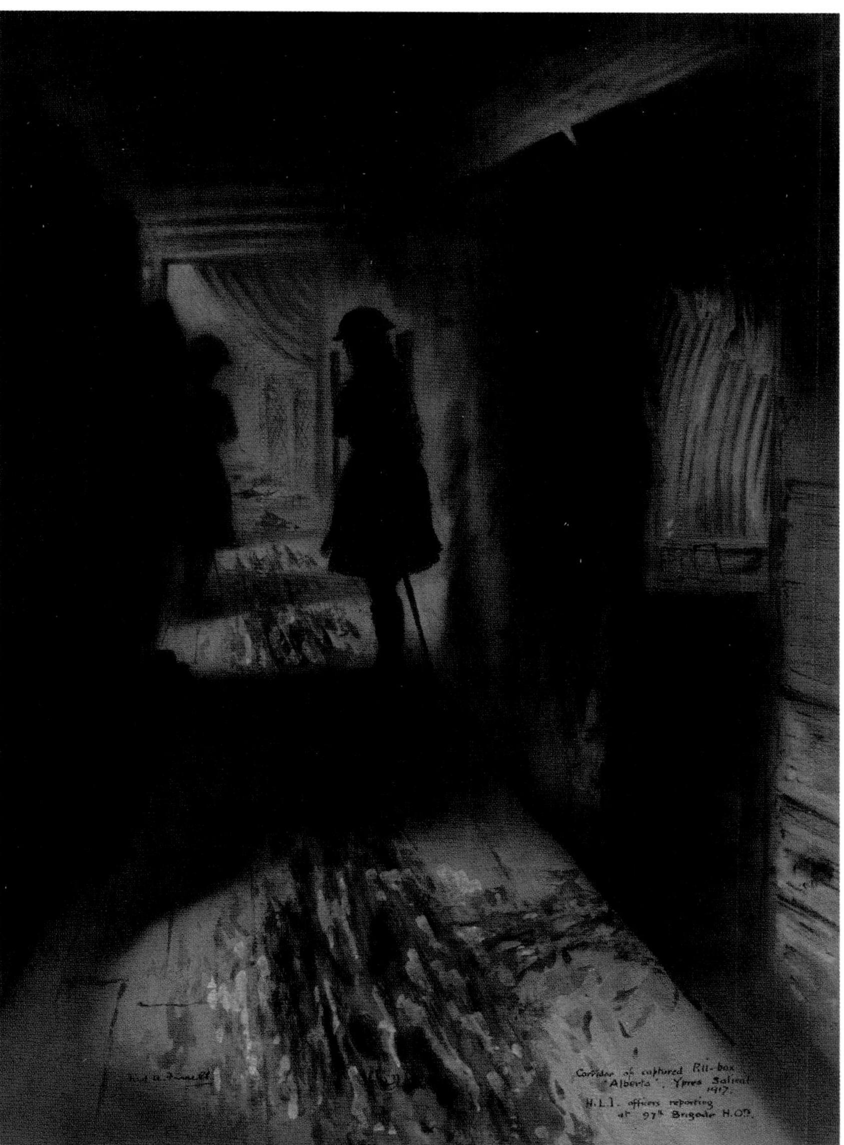

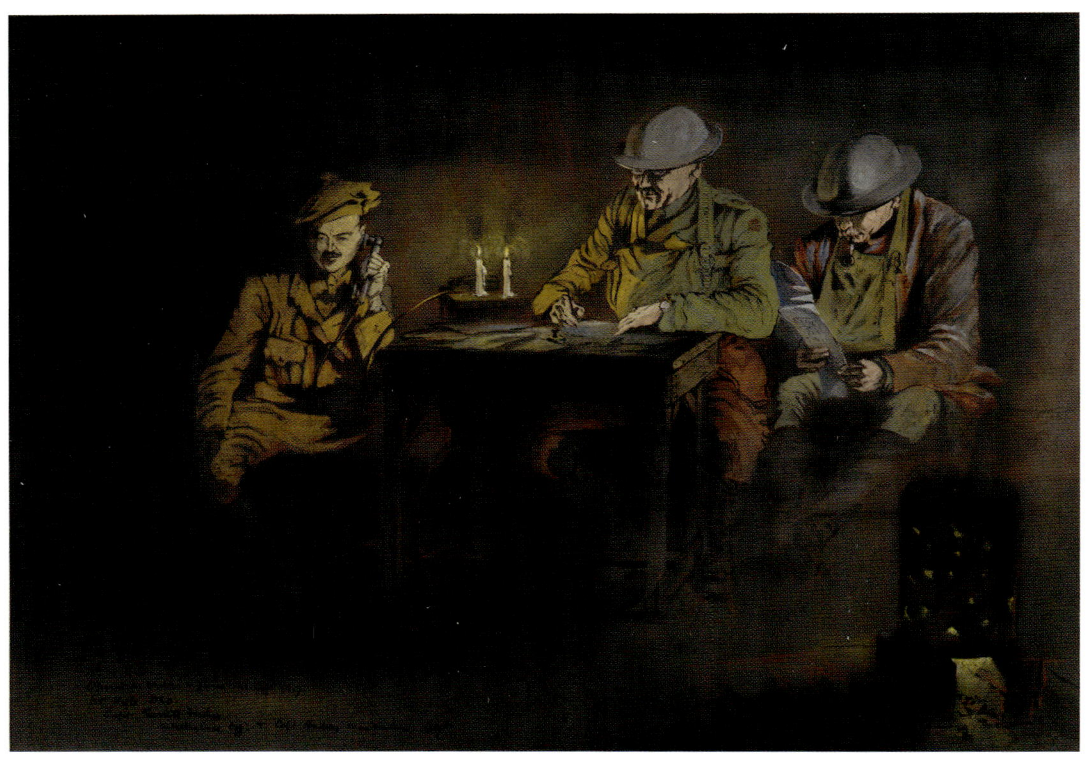

29

16th HLI (Boys Brigade Battalion) Operation Orders

Signed: 'Fred A. Farrell'
Inscriptions: '16th H.L.D./Operation
orders – Ypres Salient 1917/Col. Kyle
DSO./Capt. Garrett Fisher/Intelligence
Offr. T. Capt Andrew MacFarlane Adgt'
Watercolour and chalk on paper
PR.1921.23.au

Officers are being given orders over the
telephone. Their only light as they read
and take notes is from two candles and
the brazier that also serves to keep them
warm. The bluish tones suggest the
chill of the underground bunker. They
wear gas masks around their necks in
case of a chemical gas attack. However,
their relaxed postures, warmth of
expression and pipe-smoking, suggest a
relative state of ease.

The proportions of the figures and
their relation to each other are
slightly unnatural, reminding the
viewer that Farrell imaginatively
reconstructed scenes such as this
one, putting different figures together
from individual sketches.

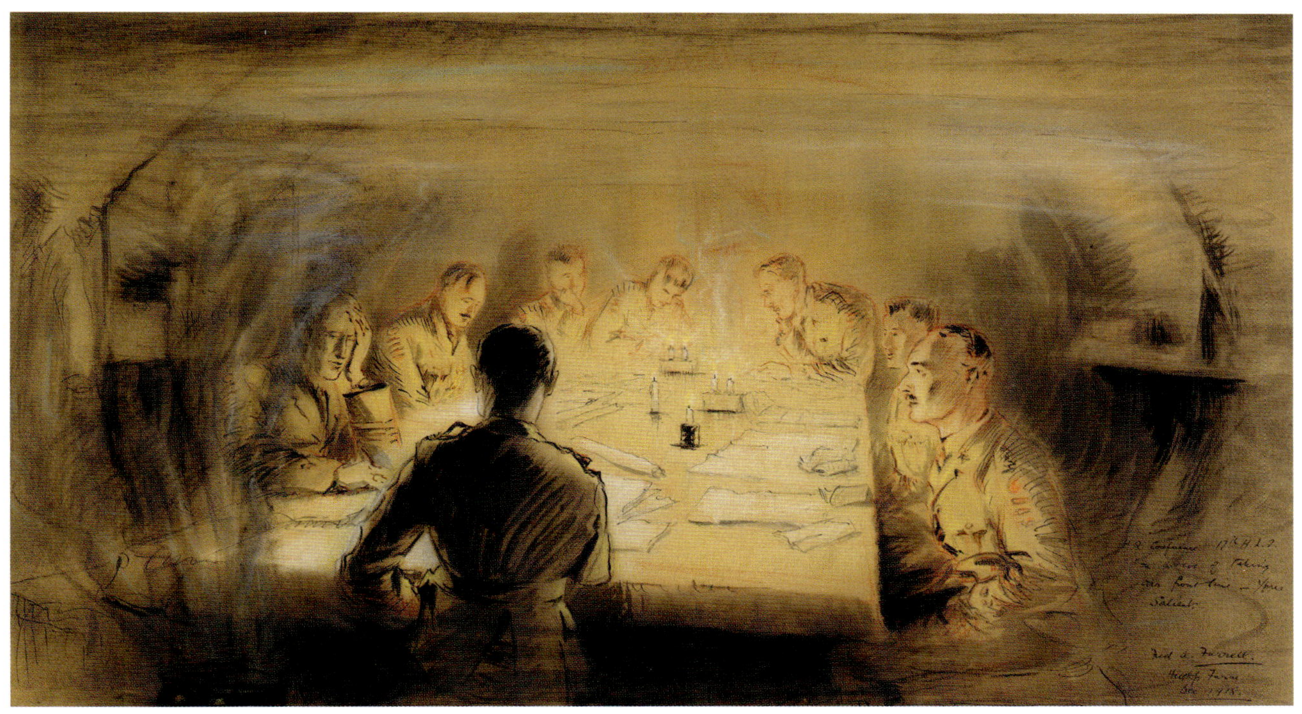

30

HQ Conference 17th HLI

Signed and dated: 'Fred A. Farrell'
Inscriptions: 'H Q. Conference
17th H.L.I. on the eve of taking over
frontline of Ypres Salient.'; 'Hilltop
Farm/Dec. 1918.'
Watercolour, ink, pencil and wash
on paper
PR.1921.23.aq

Through the curve of the corrugated
roof and the candlelight, which
highlights faces but leaves the periphery
in shadow, Farrell creates an enclosed
feeling of secrecy in this headquarters
conference. The officers of the battalion
are gathered around the table almost
in the manner of a secular Last Supper;
they seem to glow with the knowledge
and responsibility of their mission.

As the senior officer, the colonel at the
head, silhouetted and seen from behind,
benefits most from the heat of the
brazier that is positioned beside him in
the foreground. Although the drawing
is dated December 1918, the conference
would have taken place earlier, probably
in early December 1917.

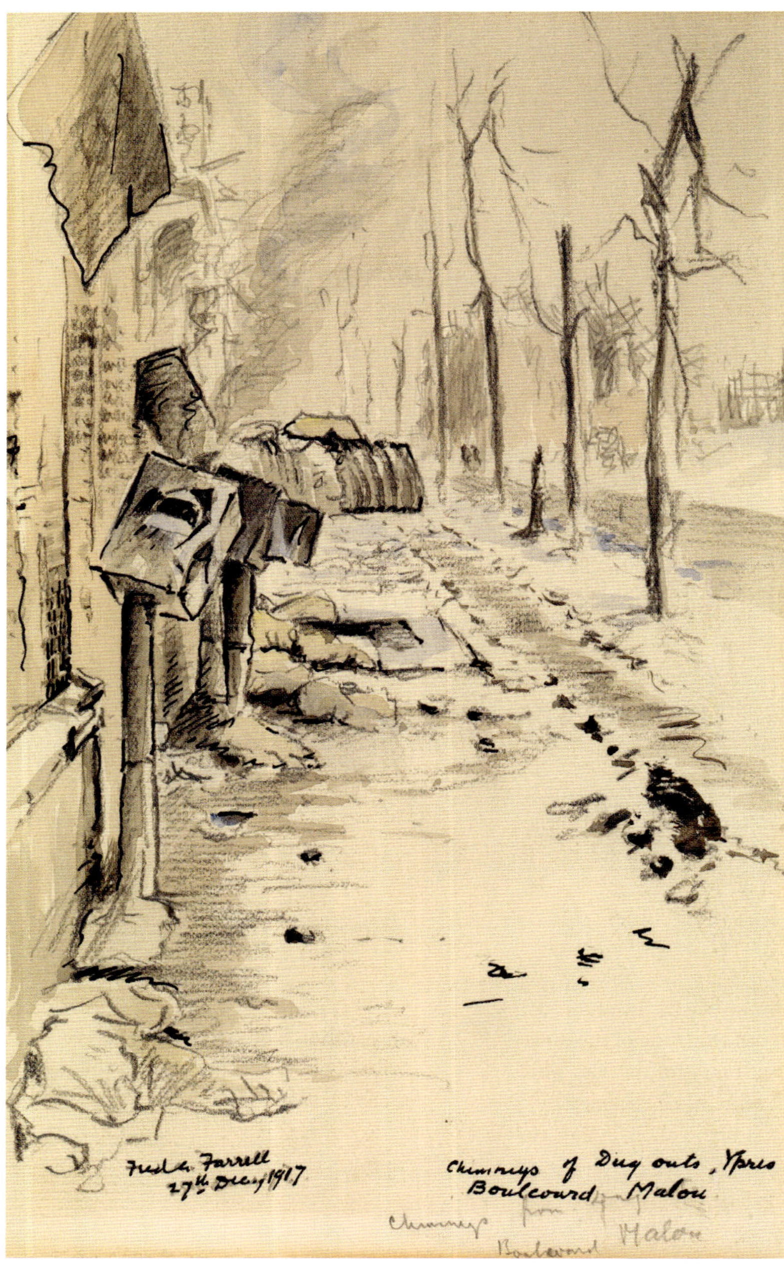

31

Chimneys of Dugouts, Ypres, Boulevard Malou

Signed and dated: 'Fred A. Farrell/
27th Dec., 1917'
Inscriptions: 'Chimneys of Dug outs,
Ypres/Boulevard Malou'; 'Chimneys
from Ypres/Boulevard Malou'
Pencil, ink, watercolour, wash on paper
PR.1921.23.ag

The great medieval cloth city of Ypres
had been at the centre of fierce fighting
since October 1914. By December
1917 most buildings above ground
were destroyed. Cellars of houses were
transformed into safe underground
dugouts for soldiers with stoves and
chimneys. The rather comical nature of
these makeshift chimneys, out of which
smoke curls, must have caught Farrell's
eye among the sandbags on this snow-
covered, formerly tree-lined, boulevard.
The row of wonky chimneys seems to
almost mirror the line of broken trees.

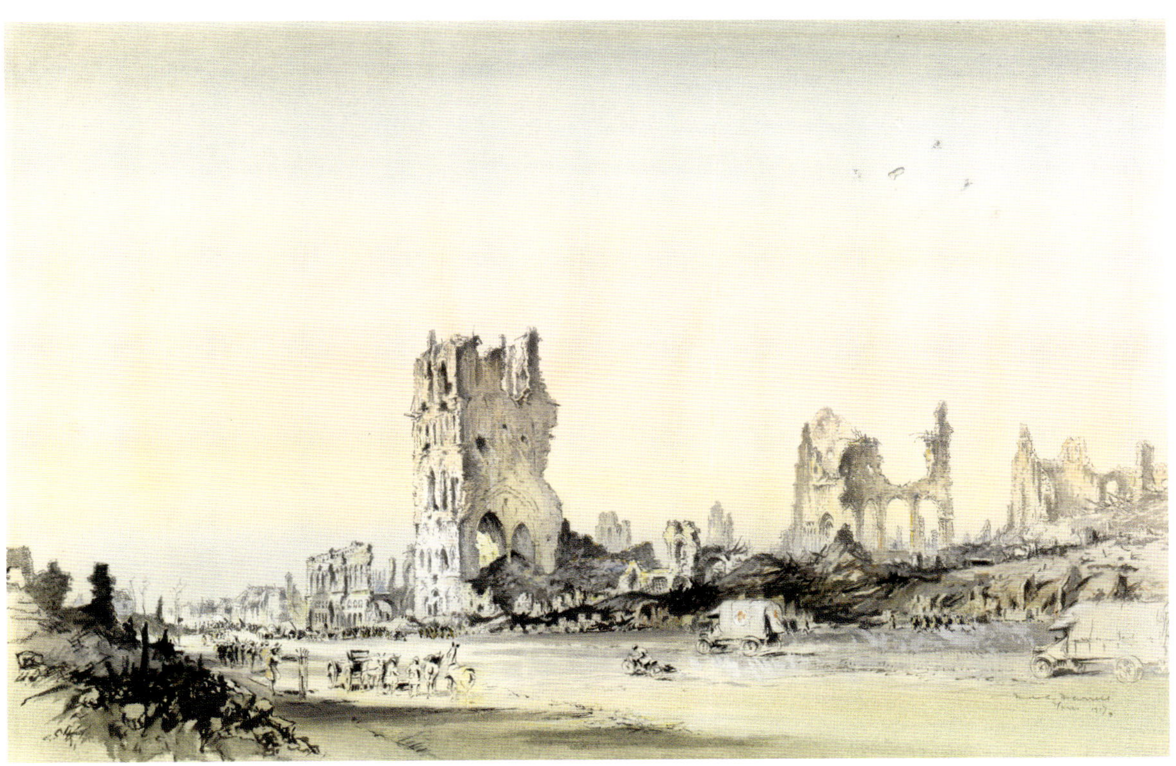

32

Ypres – Grand Place

Signed and dated: 'Fred A. Farrell,/
Ypres 1917'
Pencil and watercolour on paper
PR.1921.23.at

The Belgian city of Ypres, an important supply hub for men and materials, was devastated by shelling during the war. Here we see the dramatic ruins of the Cloth Hall, one of the most iconic landmarks of the war, which was shelled and burnt in November 1914. St Martin's Cathedral is behind. Farrell notably chose to temper the desolation of ruins and rubble with the bustle of new activity.

The road has been cleared for military traffic. A motorcycle courier speeds past an army truck and an ambulance. Soldiers march in the distance. An observation balloon and anti-aircraft fire can be seen in the sky, but the early morning light evokes hope and renewal.

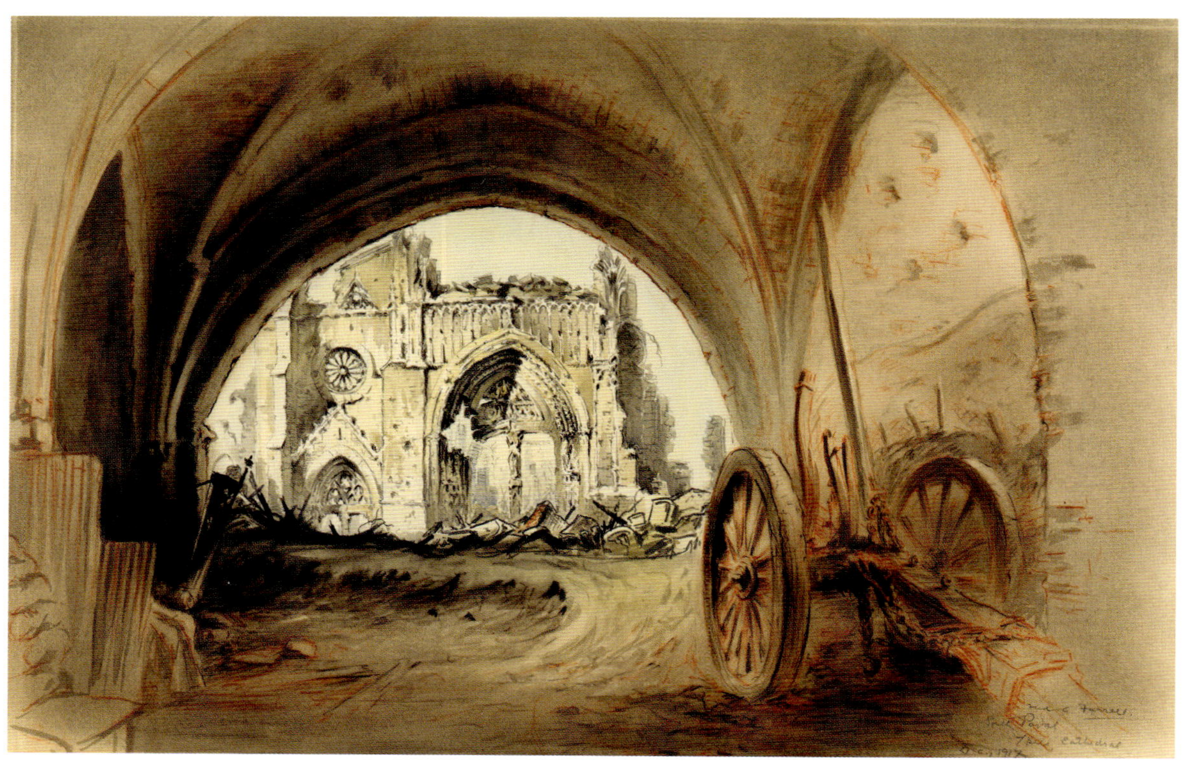

33
South Portal, Ypres Cathedral

Signed and dated: 'Fred A. Farrell.'
'Dec., 1917'
Inscriptions: 'South Portal,
Ypres Cathedral.'; 'South Portal/
Ypres Cathedral'
Watercolour, pencil and chalk
on paper
PR.1921.23.s

This view of the ruins of St Martin's
Cathedral in Ypres, seen through
a cloistered vault, is typical of
Farrell's attraction to arched format
compositions. It shows an awareness
of earlier art where doors or gateways
are often used to frame views through
to landscapes or courtyards beyond.
The arch is a particularly appropriate
framing device for this ecclesiastical
subject, although it is startlingly
juxtaposed with a gun carriage. The arch
also serves to ground the picture, giving
a firm sense of solidity which contrasts
with the ruinous remains beyond. The
message seems to be a patriotic one;
although neither roof nor walls of the
central cathedral fabric remain, a core
strength survives.

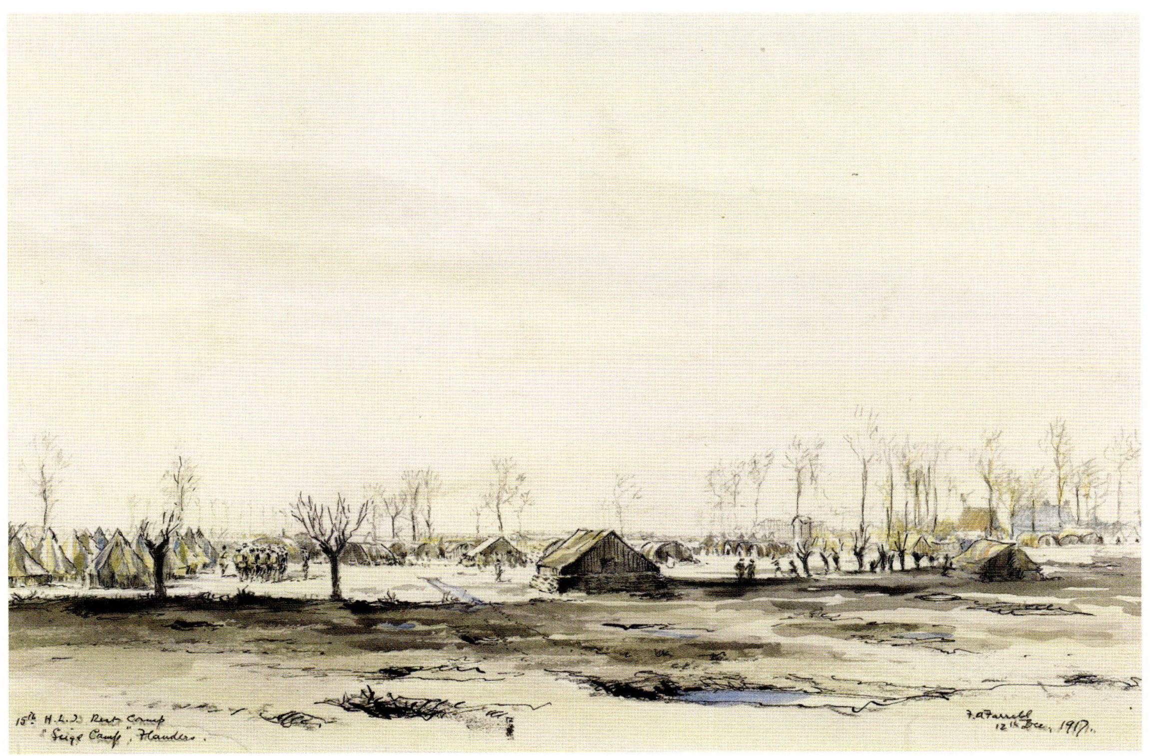

34
15th H.L.I. Rest Camp, Flanders

Signed and dated: F. A. Farrell/
12th Dec, 1917'
Inscription: '15th H.L.I. Rest
Camp/"Seige Camp", Flanders.'
Ink and watercolour on paper
PR.1921.23.ah

Troops were rotated so that they were
only on the Front Line for a few days.
When away from the line, the troops
stayed in reserve in tents or huts like
these at Siege Camp. In December 1917
the weather was poor and the water
table in Flanders was high, as can be
seen from the shell craters here. This
made conditions bad. Farrell's limited
range of colours suggests the harshness
of the weather and the surroundings.

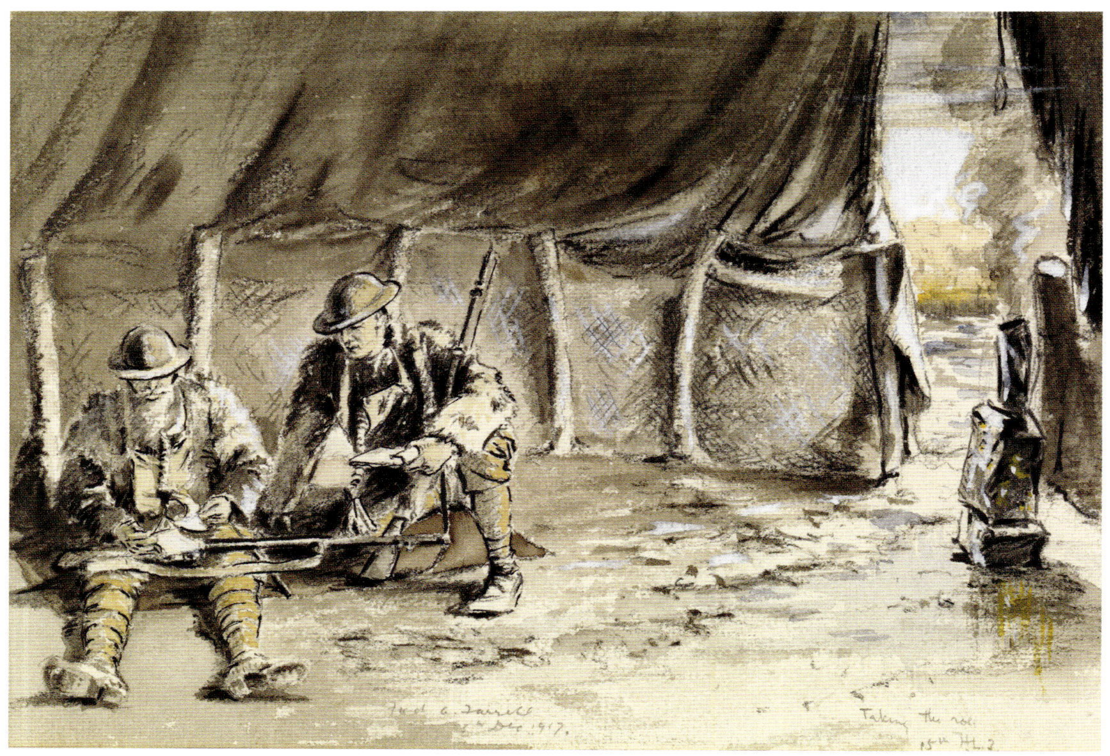

35
Taking the Roll 15th H.L.I.

Signed and dated: 'Fred A. Farrell/
23rd Dec 1917.'
Inscription: 'Taking the Roll/
15th H.L.I.'
Ink, chalk and watercolour on paper
PR.1921.23.aj

It is winter and the soldiers are wearing
sheepskin coats for warmth, and gas
masks around their necks in case of
chemical attack. The fact that they
are carrying rifles while dealing with
administrative paperwork indicates that
they are probably sergeants. The tent in
which they crouch is likely to be in a rest
area away from the Front Line. A small
stove provides a little extra heat.

They may be calculating the current
strength of the unit by counting the
men present.

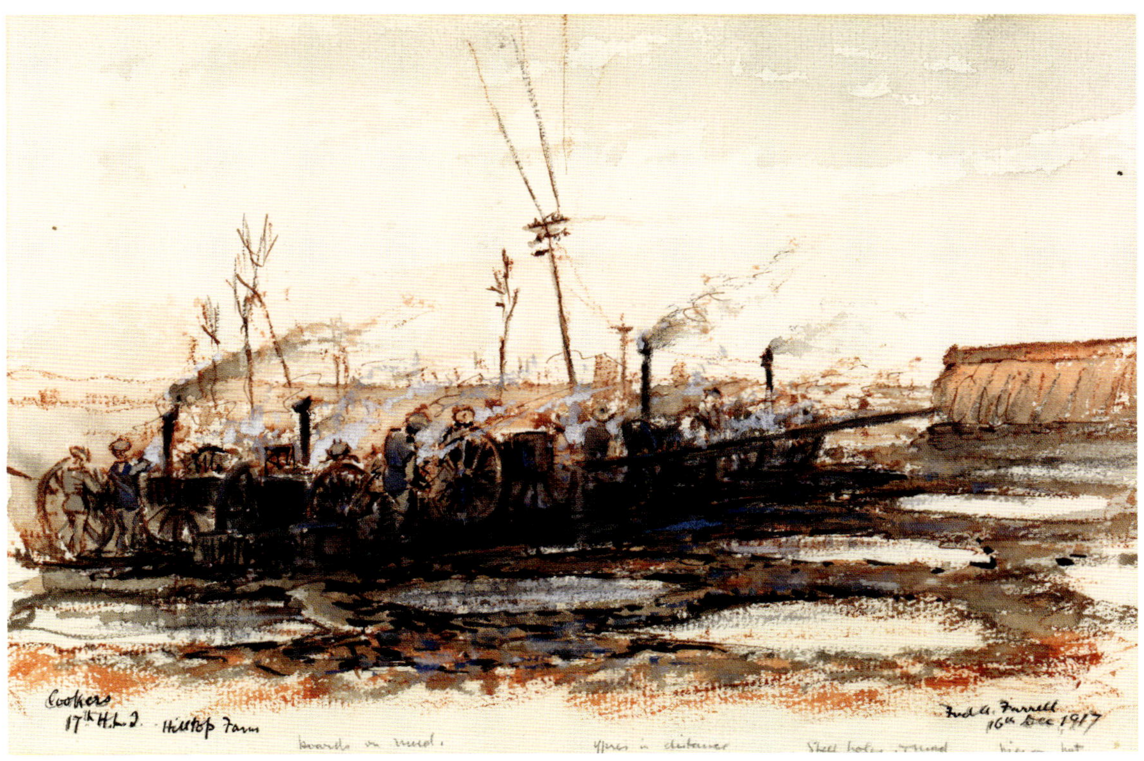

36
Cookers, 17th H.L.I., Hill Top Farm

Signed and dated: 'Fred A. Farrell/
16th Dec 1917'
Inscriptions: 'Cookers/17th H.L.I.
Hilltop Farm'; 'boards on mud.';
'Ypres in distance'; 'shell holes & mud';
'nissen hut'
Ink, chalk, watercolour, wash and
bodycolour on paper
PR.1921.23.ak

The large-wheeled contraptions with
chimneys in this image are not artillery
but mobile cookers, used to provide
the troops with warm food in the
extreme cold of the winter of 1917.
The men in Tam o' Shanter caps are
the battalion cooks struggling with
outdoor cooking on cratered ground
in poor weather conditions.

The angle of the steam and the turned
backs of the men suggest a brisk wind.
The dominating red-brown colour
scheme implies a battle against mud.
Hill Top Farm was just outside Ypres,
which can be seen in the background.

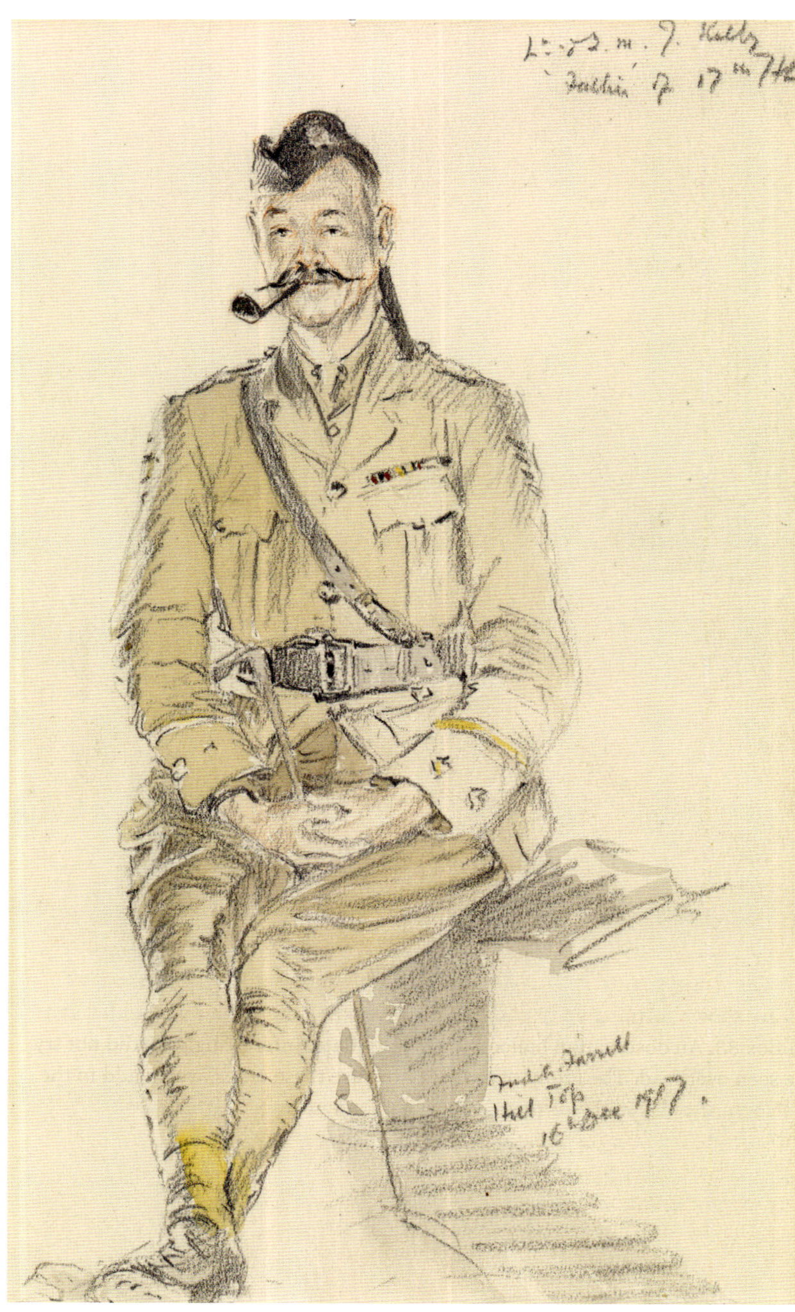

37
*Lt & QM J. Kelly, 'Father' of
17th HLI*

Signed and dated: 'Fred A. Farrell/
Hill Top/16th Dec 1917.'
Inscription: 'Lt. & QM J. Kelly,
'Father' of 17th HLI.'
Watercolour and pencil on paper
PR.1921.23.am

Kelly was an ex-Sergeant Major of
the Royal Scots who had served in
the Boer War and was a decorated
soldier. Before being made an officer
and Quartermaster he was the first
Regimental Sergeant Major of the 17th
Highland Light Infantry, a volunteer
battalion raised by Glasgow Chamber
of Commerce. He is shown in a relaxed
attitude, playfully sitting on a funnel
with his cane between his legs, smoking
a pipe. His yellow socks add a lively
splash of colour.

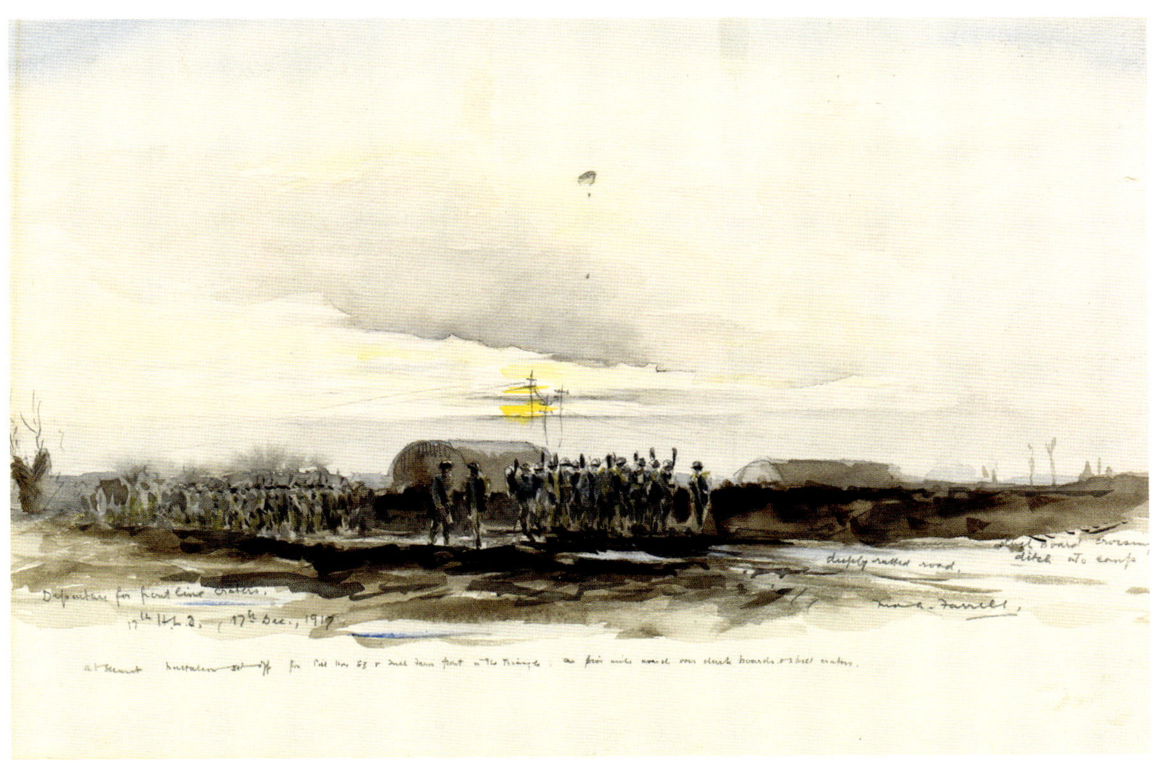

38
Departure for the Front Line

Signed: 'Fred A. Farrell.'
Inscriptions: 'Departure for front line'; 'craters'; '17th H.L.I., 17th Dec., 1917.'; 'Observation Balloon.'; 'deeply rutted road.'; 'duck board crossing ditch into camp'; 'at sunset battalion set off for Pill Box 83 & Inch Farm front in The Triangle, as prior units march over duck boards & shell craters.'
Pencil and watercolour on paper
PR.1921.23.ac

The sun sets over the rest camp at Hill Top Farm which is surrounded by waterlogged craters and ditches. The troops are shown forming up to march to Pill Box 83. An observation balloon can be seen overhead. The group of three telegraph poles in the centre of the composition, in front of the setting sun, gives the work a religious dimension, prompting reflection on the nature of sacrifice.

The pencil notations are for Farrell's benefit, to help him interpret the simple pencil drawings he made on the spot. Watercolour was added at a later date. Interestingly, he did not try to erase these notes, which add to the documentary feel.

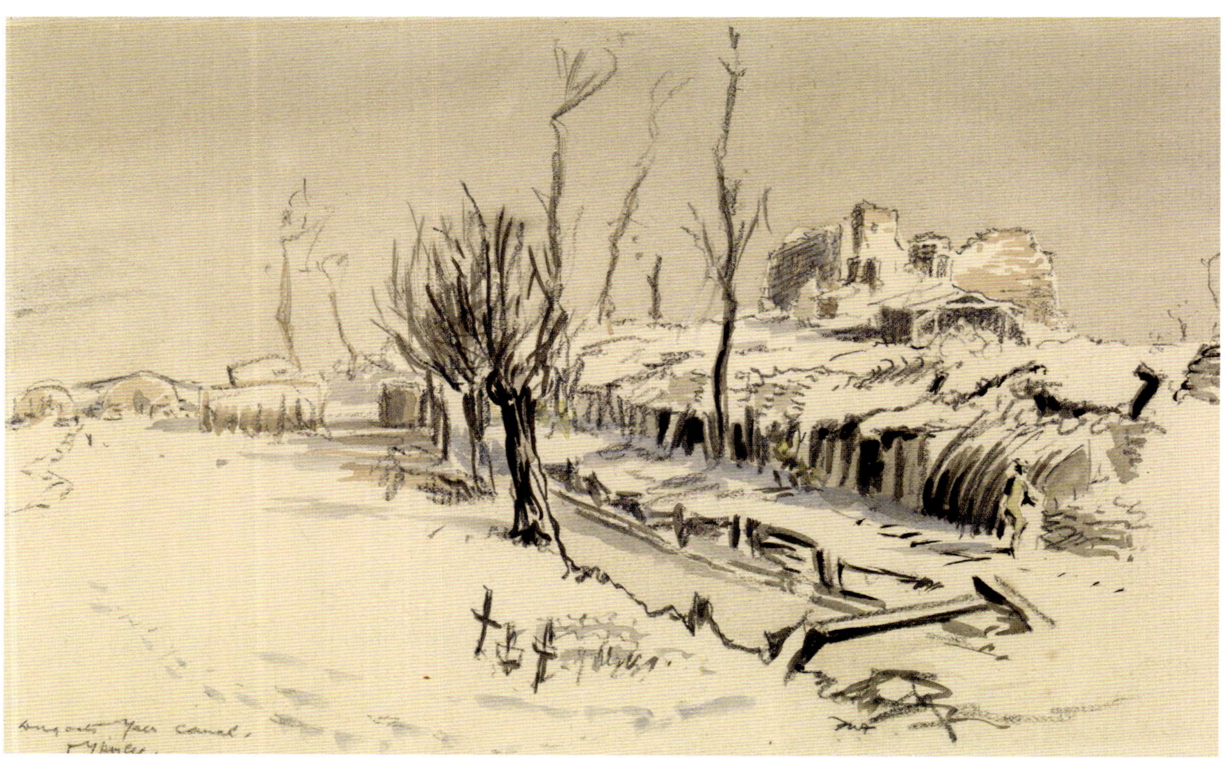

39
Dug Outs, Yser Canal and Ypres

Signed: 'FAF'
Inscriptions: 'Dug outs, Yser canal./
& Ypres.'
Chalk and watercolour on paper
PR.1921.23.ai

The Yser Canal ran to the north and west of Ypres, connecting the River Lys and the River Yser which enabled goods to be shipped to Nieuport on the coast in peacetime. This painting shows the use of the canal bank as a good place to dig safe bunkers and dugouts. Footprints lead from a makeshift bridge across the frozen canal through the snow to Nissen huts.

Ruined buildings and crosses marking the graves of the fallen remind the viewer that the landscape was the scene of former fighting. The heavy sky suggests more snow is on the way.

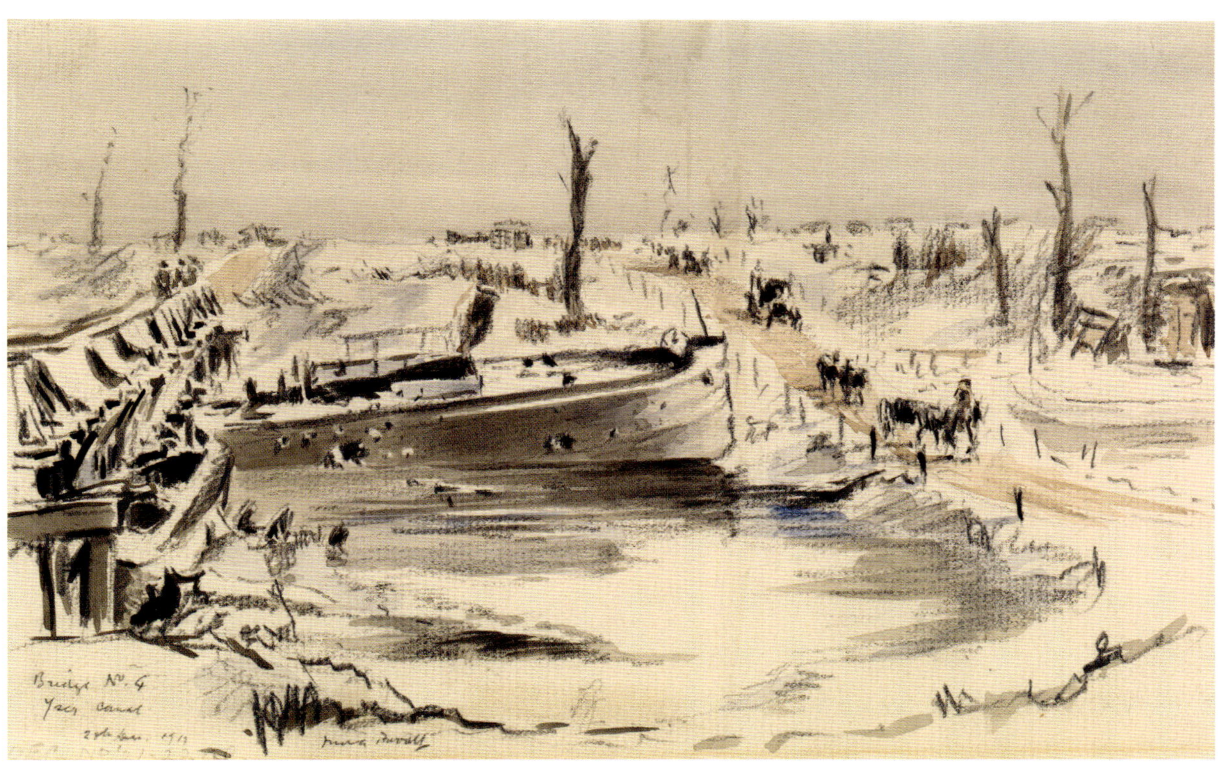

40
Yser Canal

Signed: 'Fred A Farrell'
Inscriptions: 'Bridge No. 4/
Yser canal/28th Jan 1919'
Pencil, watercolour and ink on paper
PR.1921.23.ad

On the left of the picture is Bridge 4 over the Yser Canal. As the canal had been closed to shipping since the German advance into Belgium in late 1914, an earthen causeway was built to allow traffic to cross the canal. Farrell shows this being used by horses, carts and motorized vehicles. At the centre of the composition is a forlorn, stranded boat pierced by shell holes.

Although the landscape is a bleak one, and the sky is heavy with snow, Farrell draws our attention to the activity along the roads, suggesting the resilience of the Allies.

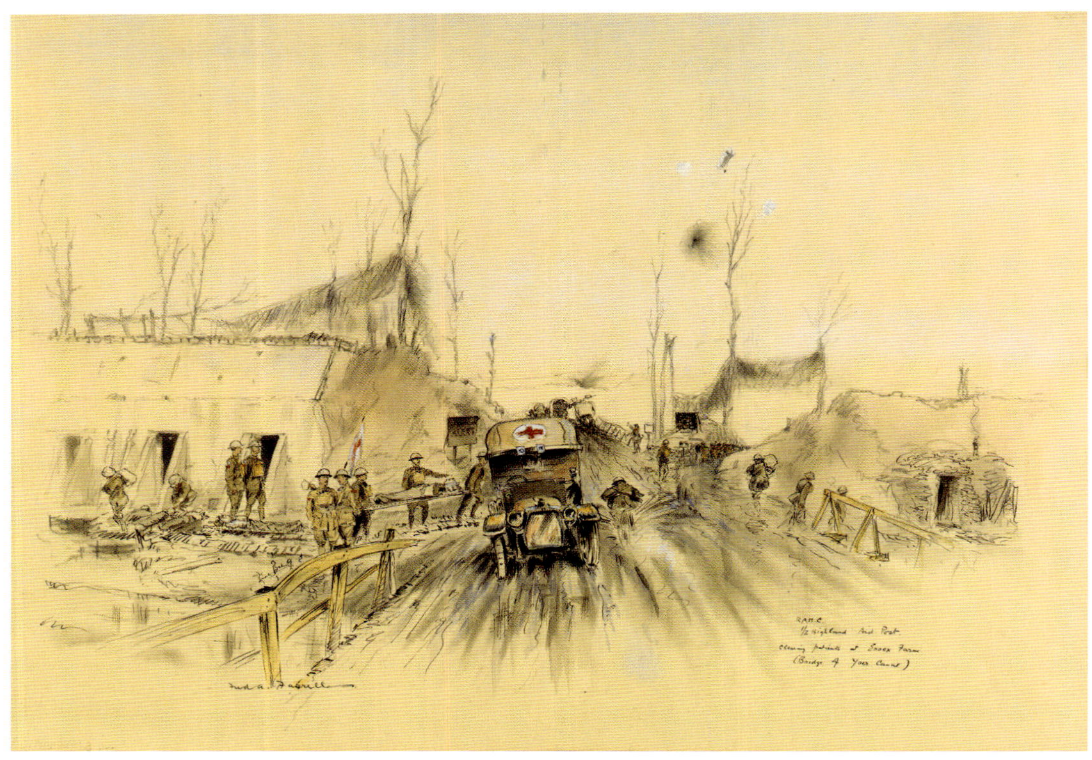

41

R.A.M.C. of the Division Loading Ambulance Cars at Essex Farm Dressing Station

Signed: 'Fred A Farrell'
Inscriptions: 'R.A.M.C./1/2 Highland
Aid Post./Clearing patients at Essex
Farm/(Bridge 4 Yser Canal)'; [on sign]
'RESPIRATORS/ALERT'
Ink, pencil and watercolour on paper
PR.1921.23.p

Essex Farm was next to Bridge 4
over the Yser Canal. Within concrete
bunkers built into an embankment
beside the canal was an Advanced
Dressing Station. It was run by a Field
Ambulance, which was not a vehicle
but a medical unit responsible for
treating and evacuating the wounded.
It sustained significant damage during
bombardments. Shells can be seen
exploding in the background, with

anti-aircraft fire overhead. The aid post
itself was located in an embankment
beside the canal. Camouflage nets
hang from trees. Stretchers are being
loaded into a motorized ambulance.
A motorcycle courier speeds past,
spraying mud in its wake. Farrell gives
a sense of movement and dynamism
through the head-on view and sharply
converging perspective.

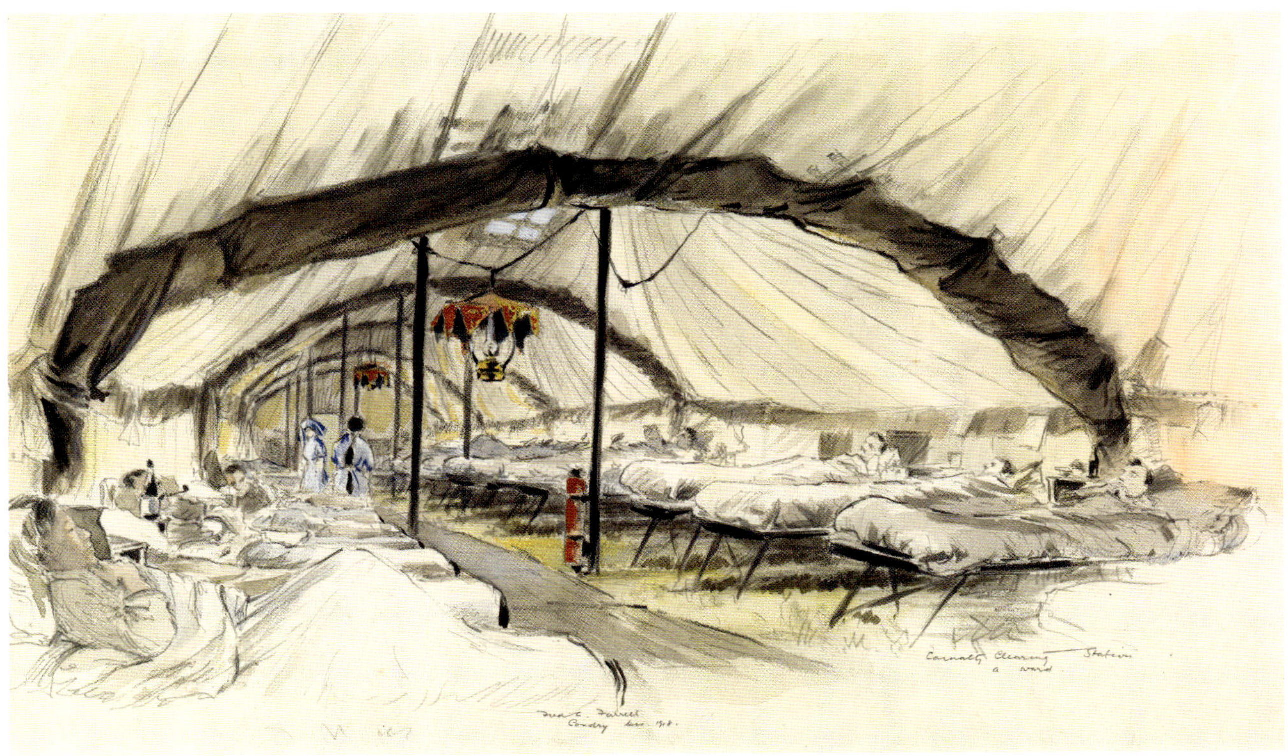

42

Tommies' Ward

Signed and dated: 'Fred A. Farrell/
Caudry Dec. 1918'
Inscriptions: 'Casualty Clearing
Station/a ward'
Pencil and watercolour on paper
PR.1921.23.h

After emergency treatment, the
Field Ambulances would transfer the
wounded to a Casualty Clearing Station,
like this one at Caudry, near Cambrai.
These were small hospitals a few miles
from the Front, just beyond the line of
fire. They were based in tents or huts
and had wards and surgical operating
theatres. This was as far forward as
nurses were stationed.

Some patients remained until they were
well enough to return to their units, the
rest until they were sufficiently stable to
be moved to larger hospitals in France or
the UK to recuperate. Some were sent to
Stobhill Hospital in Glasgow.

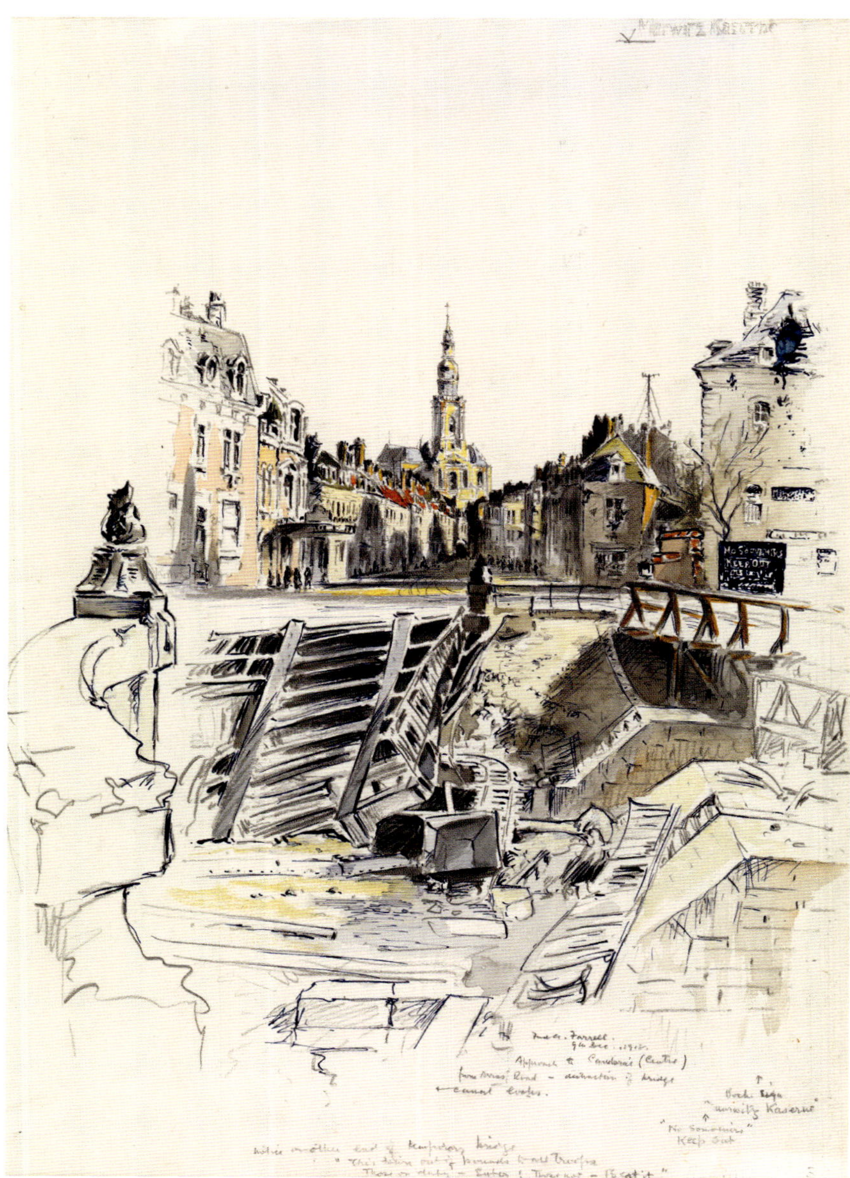

43

Entrance to Cambrai from Arras

Signed and dated: 'Fred A. Farrell./
9th Dec. 1918'
Inscriptions: 'Approach to Cambrai
(Centre) from Arras Road – destruction
of bridges and canal locks.'; 'Boche sign
"Marwitz Kaserne"/"No Souvenirs"/
Keep Out'; 'notice on other end of
temporary bridge "This town out of
bounds to all troops/Those on duty –
Enter! Those not – Beat it"'
Ink, pencil and watercolour on paper
PR.1921.23.g

Farrell contrasts the devastated canal
and destroyed bridge in the foreground
of this picture, which are depicted in a
fairly sketchy, almost monochromatic
manner, with the more detailed and
finished townscape with its signs of
reconstruction. Army engineers have
built a temporary bridge over the canal
on the right. Although many buildings
have damaged roofs, the colourful, sunlit
streets are busy with activity and suggest
renewed optimism. Signs warn looters
and troublemakers to stay away.

44

Iwuy, When the Civilians were Returning

Signed and dated: 'Fred A. Farrell/
10th Dec 1918'
Inscription: 'Boche Sentry Box at
Iwuy/1/7 Black Watch in possession'
Watercolour and chalk on paper
PR.1921.23.f

The British recaptured the French
village of Iwuy in October 1918.
Damaged roofs and glassless windows
show the devastation of the war. Soldiers
have patched up the holes so they can be
warm and dry in their billets. The green
paint used to hide the previous red,
white and black colour scheme of the
German sentry box is being washed off
in the rain. The Black Watch soldier on
duty is shown standing relaxed but alert.
Farrell again focuses on reconstruction,
showing owners of houses returning to
reclaim their properties.

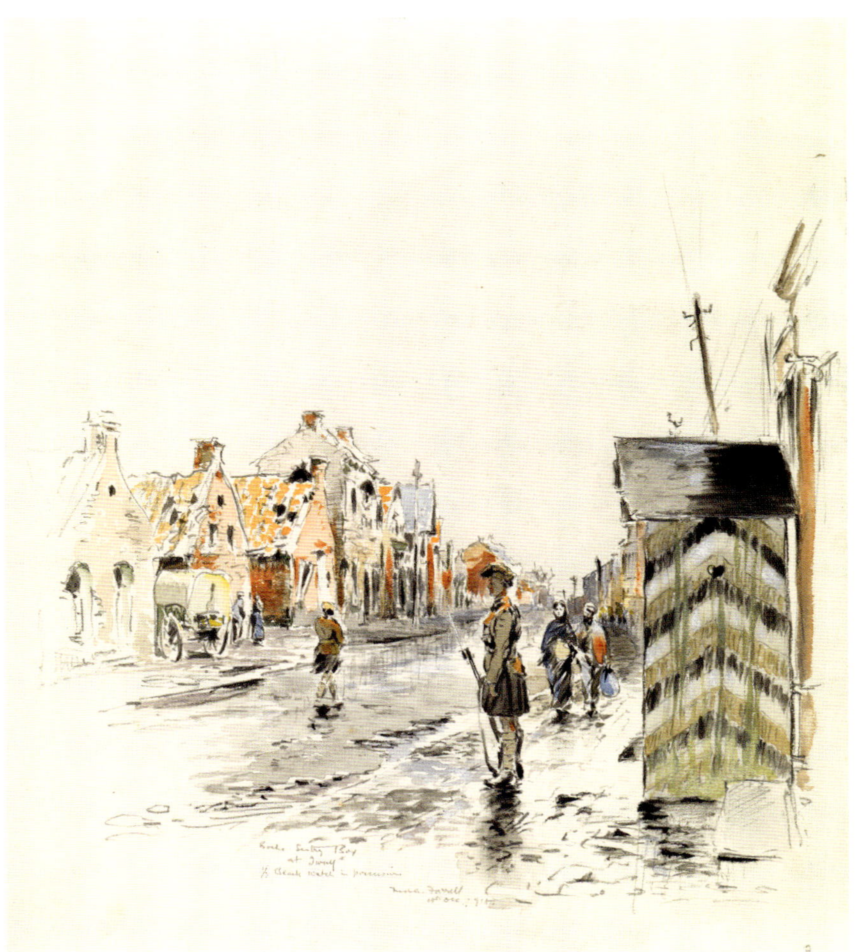

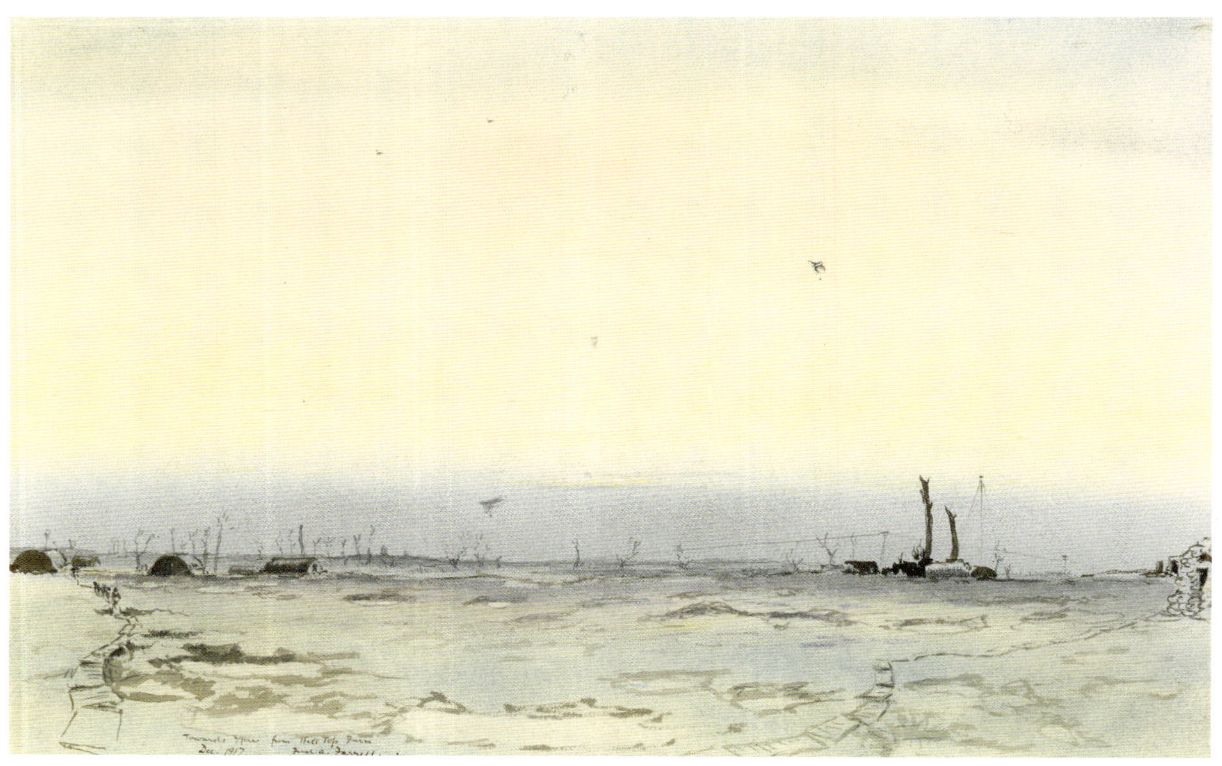

45

Towards Ypres from Hill Top Farm

Signed and dated: 'Dec. 1917.
Fred A. Farrell.'
Inscription: 'Towards Ypres from
Hill Top Farm'
Pencil and watercolour on paper
PR.1921.23.x

This bleak winter landscape with its blasted trees and cratered ground is a powerful reminder of the consequences of war. Duckboards lead the eye out over the frozen wasteland to groups of Nissen huts and vehicles, obviously a rest area, now behind the lines. Overhead, biplanes and observation balloons dot the sky. Farrell uses cool blues and yellows to suggest the deep freeze of winter.

More than two-thirds of this work is sky. The whole is enigmatic and quietly atmospheric.

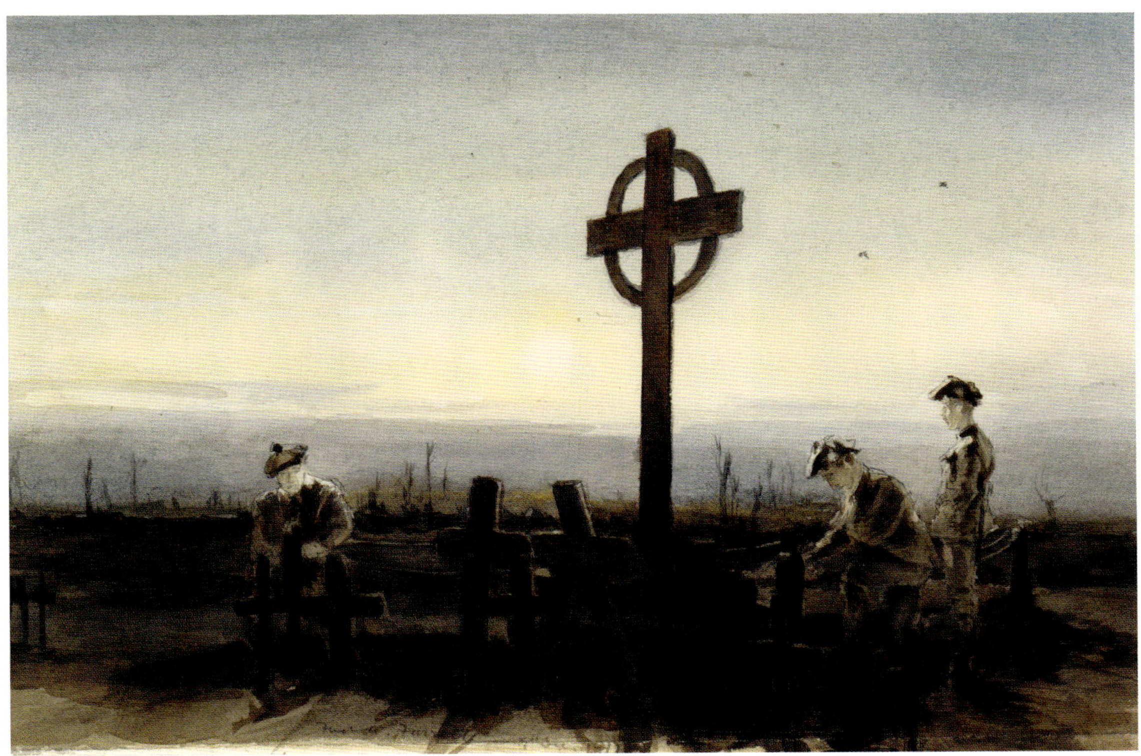

46

Graves

Signed and dated: 'Fred A. Farrell/
19th Dec. 1917'
Inscriptions: 'Graves'; 'In memory
of the Officers, N.C.O.s, 16th Bn HLI,
killed in action on Passchendaele
ridge 2nd/12/17'; 'Not in Vain';
'Sgt. Colin Turner.'
Watercolour on paper
PR.1921.23.al

This is a moving and reflective image
of soldiers visiting the graves of their
recently fallen comrades. The central
memorial solemnly stands out against
a barren, denuded landscape and a cold
winter sky. Farrell again sets the scene at
evening to suggest not only the end of a
day, but the end of individual lives.

The operation at Passchendaele Ridge,
which led to the massacre of British
soldiers, was unusual in that it took
place at night. Wooden crosses were put
on graves until the Imperial War Graves
Commission replaced them with stone.

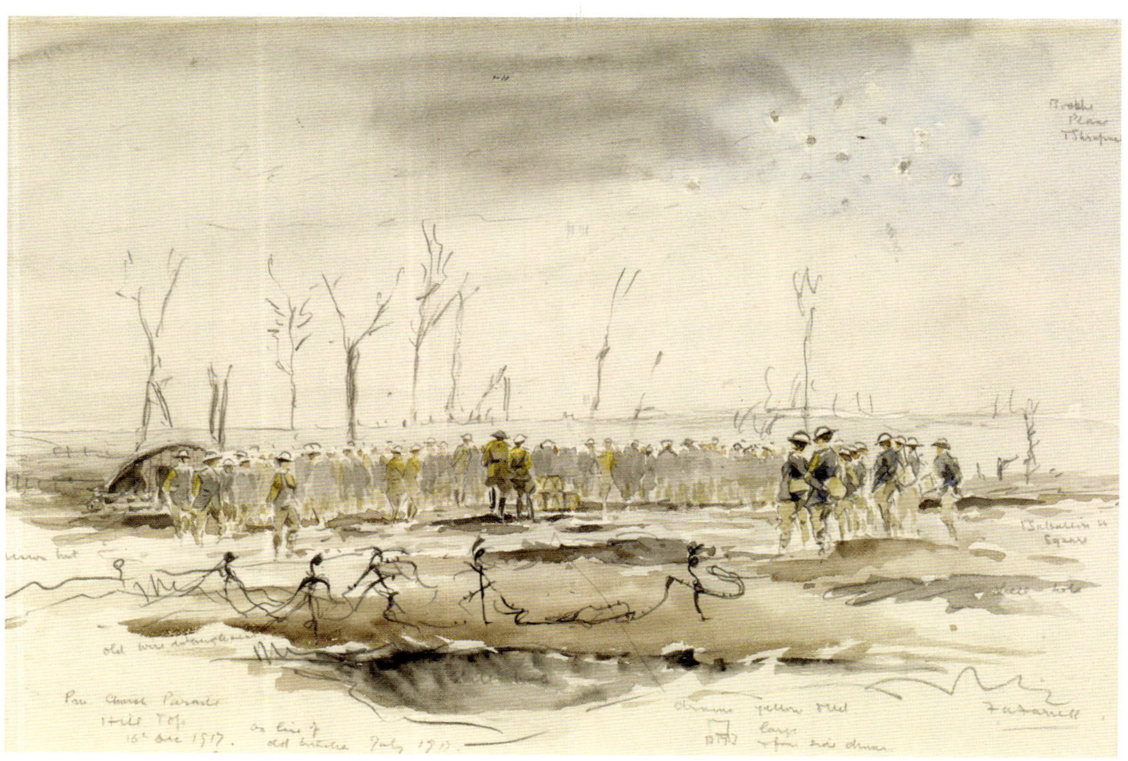

47

Church Parade, Hill Top

Signed: 'F. A. Farrell'
Inscriptions: 'Pm Church Parade/
Hill Top/16th Dec 1917.'; 'On line
of old trenches July 1917.'; 'old wire
entanglement'; 'nissen hut'; 'drums
yellow mid/large/& four side drums.';
'shell hole'; 'shell hole'; 'Battalion in
square'; 'Bosche Plane & Schrapnel"
'Cap. Rev [?]. S. [?]man/17th H.L.I.'
Pencil, chalk and watercolour on paper
PR.1921.23.af

A simple church service takes place
at Hill Top Farm, north east of Ypres.
Regimental drums have been piled to
form a makeshift altar, and men gather
with their heads respectfully bowed.
Now behind the Allied lines, the farm
was the scene of former fighting.

The landscape around about is marred
by barbed wire, craters and bare broken
trees. Overhead aerial shell bursts mark
the flight of planes.

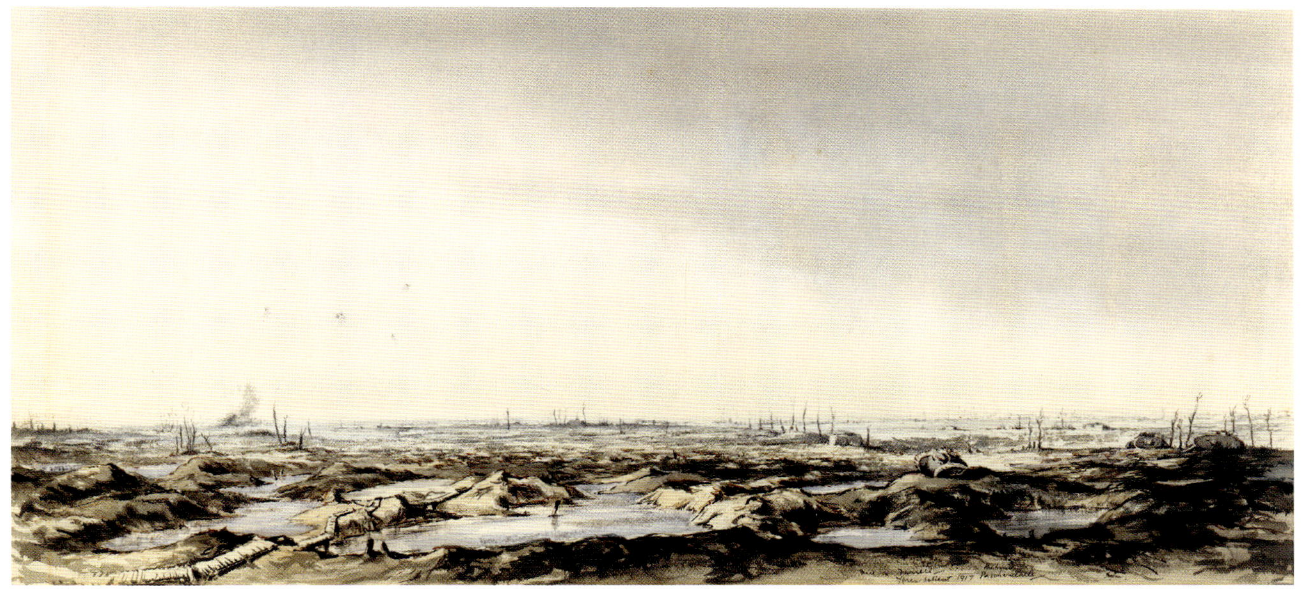

48

Ypres Salient 1917 – Behind Passchendaele

Signed: 'Fred A. Farrell'
Inscription: 'Ypres salient 1917/
Behind Passchendaele'
Watercolour and ink on paper
PR.1921.23.ap

This desolate image of a land ravaged and made unrecognizable by war is troubling and powerful. Although devoid of human life, the trauma of the soil here speaks of distress and suffering on a human level. Violence is all around. Stumps of trees stab the sky. Duckboards wind their way around water-filled shell holes that now form death traps.

Shells explode in the distance. The expressionless skies seem to be in mourning with the landscape.

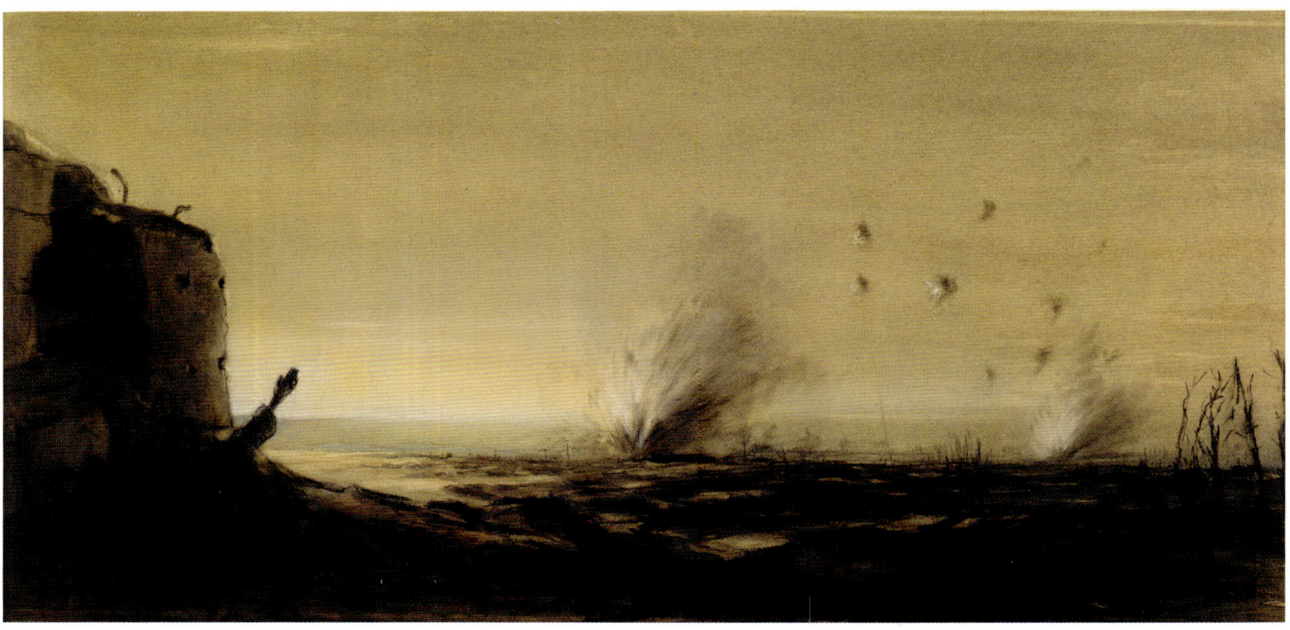

49
Battlefield

Signed and dated: 'F. A. Farrell 1917'
Watercolour and chalk on paper
PR.1921.23.aw

The arm from a statue of the crucified Christ is dramatically silhouetted among the ruins of a destroyed church. Shells burst on formerly fertile farmland, now a battlefield. The retreating German army tactically destroyed buildings in their wake. Their particular technique for churches was to blow up the roof and allow the west door and tower to fall into the nave.

As a propaganda strategy war artists often emotively depicted the desecration of churches as evidence of the enemy's depravity. The setting sun adds further poignancy to this image.

50
Hung Up!

Signed: 'F. A. F.'
Inscription: 'Hung Up!'
Watercolour and ink on paper
PR.1921.23.an

This is a disturbing image of a dead
soldier caught on barbed wire, his gun
and helmet on the ground in front of
him. The physical gloom complements
the darkness of the subject; the limp
body is eerily highlighted by a passing
flare. The title is an uncomfortable
example of macabre trench humour.
It is comparable in subject matter to
C.R.W. Nevinson's controversial painting
Paths of Glory (1917, Imperial War
Museum), which was famously censored
when it was exhibited at the Leicester
Galleries in 1918. It is a striking choice
for the Corporation of Glasgow's
collection of war art – it was probably
not finished until after the war and
therefore escaped censorship.

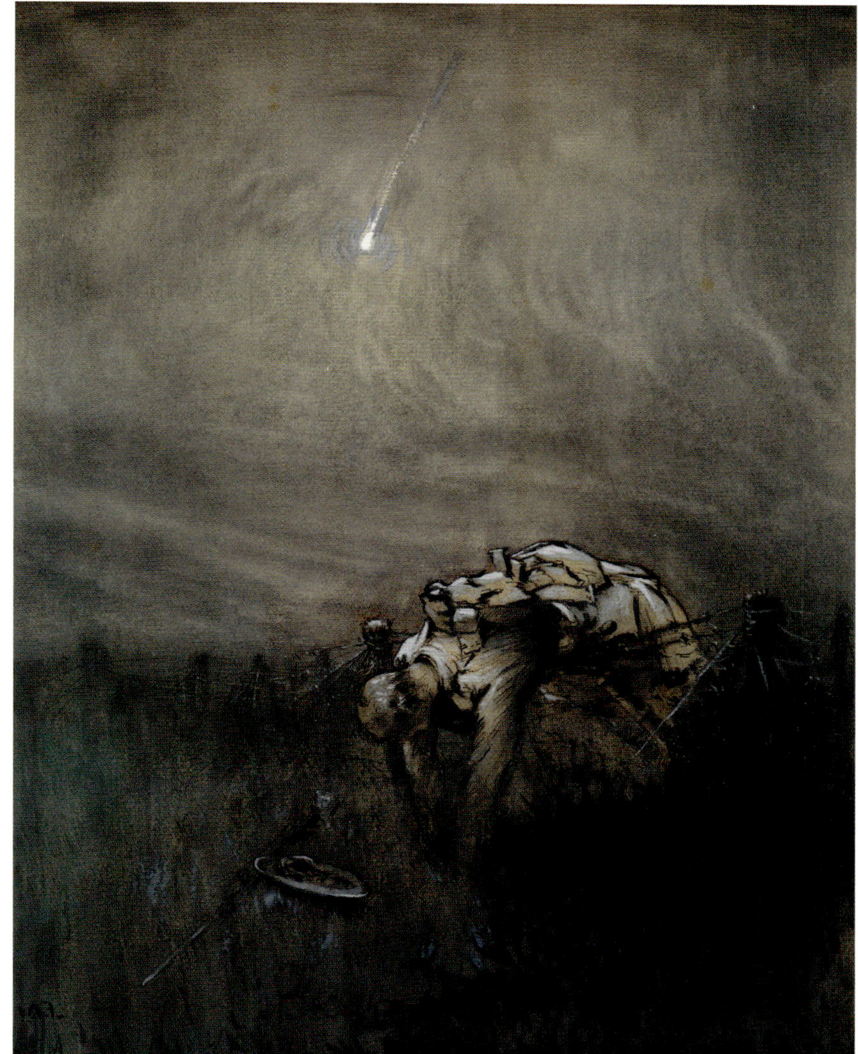

Notes

Chapter 1

1 Lord Provost Sir Thomas Dunlop to Lieutenant Colonel John Buchan, Director of Information, War Office, London SW1, 20 June 1917 (*Lord Provost Letter Book*, 1st June 1917 to 1st Oct. 1917, Glasgow City Archives, Mitchell Library, G1.1.48, pp. 113–14).

2 John Bradbury to Minister of Information, 24 August 1918 (National Archives, London, T1/12216).

3 'Mr. Joseph Pennell's War Lithographs', *Glasgow Herald*, 27 January 1917, p. 8c.

4 'London Correspondence. Local War Museums', *Glasgow Herald*, 6 March 1917, p. 5a.

5 'Local War Museums. The Glasgow Collection', *Glasgow Herald*, 7 March 1917, p. 8b.

6 'The 51st Division: War Drawings by Mr. Fred Farrell', *Glasgow Herald*, 30 April 1920, p. 8h.

7 *Glasgow Bulletin*, 1 May 1920.

8 Lord Provost Thomas Dunlop to Hon. Ian Macpherson, MP, Under Secretary for Warm [sic], War Office, London SW, 16 March 1917 (*Lord Provost Office Correspondence*, 5th Feb. 1917 to 1st June 1917, Glasgow City Archives, Mitchell Library, G1.1.46, pp. 314–16).

9 *Ibid.*

10 'The Lord Provost. Notable Civic Career. Presentation of Portrait to Sir Thomas Dunlop', *Glasgow Herald*, 6 November 1917, p. 5c.

Chapter 2

1 *British Propaganda During the War, 1914–1918*, Secret (National Archives, London, INF 4/4A).

2 Alfred Yockney, letter template to artists, 20 August 1918 (National Archives, London, T1/12216).

3 Ministry of Information papers (National Archives, London, T1/12216).

4 Minutes of the Corporation of the City of Glasgow and Committees. At a special meeting of the Committee on Parks, Gardens & Galleries, 28 October 1918, Print No. 27, p. 2100, issued 11 November 1918, in *Minutes of the Corporation of Glasgow, April 1918 to Nov 1918*, Glasgow Museums Archives.

5 1881 Scotland Census; 1891 Scotland Census; 1901 Scotland Census; Birth Certificate, Frederick Arthur Farrell (www.ancestry.co.uk). Post Office Directory, 1818–1819.

6 'Exhibition Builders No. 12 – Ex-Bailie Dunlop, Scottish Modern Fine Art', *Daily Record*, 1 February 1911, p. 3d. 'Mr. Dunlop's Career', *Glasgow Herald*, 6 November 1914, p. 4a-b.

7 See Chapter 1, note 8.

8 Fred A. Farrell, *Lady Cawely* (no. 136), Gallery IX: Artists in Black and White, *Scottish Exhibition of National History, Art and Industry, Glasgow, 1911: Official Catalogue of the Fine Arts Section*, Dalross Ltd, Glasgow, 1911, p. 76.

9 Roger Billcliffe, *The Royal Glasgow Institute of the Fine Arts 1861–1989: A Dictionary of Exhibitors at the Annual Exhibitions of the Royal Glasgow Institute of the Fine Arts*, 4 vols, The Woodend Press, Glasgow, 1992, vol. 2 (E–K), p. 34. British Army WWI Pension Records 1914–1920, The National Archives, London.

10 'The 51st Division: War Drawings by Mr. Fred Farrell', *Glasgow Herald*, 30 April 1920, p. 8h.

11 *Ibid.*

12 Obituary, *Glasgow Herald*, 23 April 1935, p. 9e.

13 See Chapter 1, note 8.

14 See Chapter 1, note 1.

15 C.R.W. Nevinson to Charles F.G. Masterman, 30 July 1917 (Tate Archives, London, TGA 724/9).

16 Lord Provost Thomas Dunlop to Fred A. Farrell, Glasgow Art Club, 185 Bath Street, 14 March 1917 (*Lord Provost Office Correspondence*, 5th Feb. 1917 to 1st June 1917, Glasgow City Archives, Mitchell Library, G1.1.46, p. 290). See also Chapter 1, note 8.

17 'The War and Art. "The Western Front" Drawings. (From our Correspondent.) London', *Glasgow Herald*, 23 January 1917, p. 9d.

18 'Lieut. Bone's Drawings at the Front', *Glasgow Herald*, 7 March 1917, p. 6e. 'Lieut. Bone's Drawings at the Front', *Glasgow Herald*, 8 March 1917, p. 6f.

19 'The Spirit of Pity', *Glasgow Herald*, 28 March 1917, p. 6g.

20 Farrell to Lord Provost Thomas Dunlop, 5 February 1917, Minutes of the Corporation of the City of Glasgow and Committees, 2 March 1917, Print No. 10, p. 747 in *Minutes of the Corporation of Glasgow, Nov 1916 to April 1917*. Lord Provost Thomas Dunlop to Fred A. Farrell, Art Club, 185 Bath Street, 6 February 1917 (*Lord Provost Office Correspondence*, 5th Feb. 1917 to 1st June 1917, Glasgow City Archives, Mitchell Library, G1.1.46, p. 22).

21 Elizabeth Robins Pennell, *The Life and Letters of Joseph Pennell*, 2 vols, Ernest Benn Ltd, London, 1930, vol. 2, p. 175.

22 Minutes of the Corporation of the City of Glasgow and Committees, 18 October 1917, Print No. 27, p. 2005, para c, in *Minutes of the Corporation of Glasgow, April 1917 to Nov 1917*, Glasgow Museums Archives.

23 Major A.N. Lee to Alfred Yockney, 3 April 1918 (Tate Archives, London, TGA 724/14).

24 Charles F.G. Masterman, *Report of the Work of the Bureau established for the Purpose of Laying before Neutral Nations and the Dominions the Case of Great Britain and her Allies*, 7 June 1915, p. 2 (National Archives, London, PRO, INF 4/5).

25 Lord Provost Sir Thomas Dunlop to The Most Honourable The Marquess of Graham, R.N.V.R. Headquarters, Govan, 24 July 1917 (*Lord Provost Letter Book, 1st June 1917 to 1st Oct. 1917*, Glasgow City Archives, Mitchell Library, G1.1.48, pp. 394–96).

Chapter 3

1 *Souvenir of Cardonald National Projectile Factory*, private subscription, p. 24

2 *Ibid.*, pp. 6–7.

3 *Ibid.*, p. 8.

4 *Ibid.*, p. 24.

5 See Chapter 2, note 22.

Appendix: Archival Sources Related to Fred A. Farrell

The following are letters, minutes and newspaper articles relating to Farrell's 1917 commission by the Corporation of Glasgow to produce 50 war drawings of the Home Front and Front Line.

Lord Provost Sir Thomas Dunlop to Hon Ian Macpherson, MP, Under Secretary for Warm [sic], War Office, London SW, 16 March 1917 (***Lord Provost Office Correspondence, 5th Feb. 1917 to 1st June 1917***, **Glasgow City Archives, Mitchell Library, G1.1.46, pp. 314–16**).

Dear Mr. Macpherson,

I have been approached by several representative Members of the Corporation of this City as to the propriety of Mr. Fred A. Farrell, a young but distinguished local Black and White Artist, and the son of a very esteemed citizen, proceeding to France for the purpose of obtaining, on behalf of the Corporation, a set of War Drawings and Sketches for the City's permanent connection [sic] of pictures to be housed at our Art Galleries in Kelvingrove. It is intended that the record of the Drawings and Sketches will deal with the good work of the Highland Brigade and will be made specially applicable to the Battalions of the H.L.I. that the Corporation raised at the beginning of the War. To enable Mr. Farrell to do that work it is, of course, necessary that he should receive official permission from your Department so that on his arrival at and temporary stay in France he, without being in the way, should be afforded reasonable facilities.

Along with the other Members of the Corporation I strongly approve of the proposal which has, I believe, already been carried out on behalf of the City of London by Mr. Muirhead Bone, and in a recent issue of the *Glasgow Herald* the London Correspondent of that paper urged on provincial Local Authorities to make similar arrangements as far as they could in regard to their own Districts and the special Battalions or Units connected therewith.

Such a collection of Drawings and Sketches applicable to our City Battalions would be very highly appreciated and prized not only by the Corporation but also, I am satisfied, by the general body of the people, who are all, more or less, related to the Members composing those Battalions.

In the whole circumstances I, as representing the Corporation, make the request to you, and I sincerely trust that you will favourably entertain the proposal to grant Mr. Farrell the required permission. From what I know of Mr. Farrell I am quite sure that he would produce most creditable work and would take the greatest possible care to strictly conform to any conditions that your Department might think fit to attach to the necessary permission.

I am,
Yours sincerely,
Thomas Dunlop

Lord Provost Sir Thomas Dunlop to Lieutenant Colonel Buchan, Director of Information, War Office, London, SW1, 20 June 1917 (***Lord Provost Letter Book, 1st June 1917 to 1st Oct. 1917***, **Glasgow City Archives, Mitchell Library, G1.1.48, pp. 113–14**).

My dear Sir,

On 16th. March last I wrote Mr. Ian Macpherson, Under Secretary for War, asking permission for Mr. Fred Farrel [sic], local Black and White Artist, proceeding to France for the purpose of obtaining, on behalf of the Corporation of this City, a set of War Drawings and Sketches for the City's permanent Collection of pictures to be housed in our Art Galleries at Kelvingrove, and for your information I enclose herewith copy of that letter and of subsequent letters between Mr. Macpherson and me, and also copies of letters that have passed between Sir John Lindsay, our Town-Clerk, and the Under Secretary for Scotland.

In the last letter received by me from Mr. Macpherson, that of date 14th. current, he informs me that the Prime Minister has now appointed you to deal with such matters as the application I have made, and, therefore, I now write you submitting the application, in the earnest hope that it will be favourably entertained by you.

I need not argue the case at any length as it is wholly contained in the correspondence. I think however, I should remind you of the extraordinary response this City has made in connection with the War in its contributions of men, munitions and money, and I would only emphasise what the Town-Clerk says in his letter to the Under Secretary for Scotland of 7th. April last that Mr. Farrell has been discharged from the Army; that under the provisions of the recent Military Act he cannot be recalled for further examination until the end of November next, being one year from the date of his discharge; and that accordingly there is, in the interim, time for Mr. Farrell carrying out the proposed work on behalf of the Corporation.

I sincerely trust that on consideration of the case you may see your way to grant the permission sought which would, I assure you, be highly appreciated by the Corporation and our fellow-citizens here.

I am,
My dear Sir,
Yours faithfully,
Thomas Dunlop
Lord Provost.

Lord Provost Sir Thomas Dunlop to The Most Honourable The Marquess of Graham, R.N.V.R. Headquarters, Govan, 24 July 1917 (***Lord Provost Letter book, 1st June 1917 to 1st Oct. 1917***, **Glasgow City Archives, Mitchell Library, G1.1.48, pp. 394–96**).

My Lord Marques [sic]

May I venture to briefly encroach on your valuable time by asking you to read the enclosed copies of letters of date 16th. March and 20th. June last addressed by me to Mr. MacPherson the Under Secretary for War, and to Lieutenant Colonel Buchan, the Director of Information, respectively.

On 22nd. ultimo Lieutenant Colonel Buchan wrote me as follows:– "I hope to get our accommodation for Artists at the front extended and so expedite Mr. Farrell's visit. In any case I hope to be able to fit him in before he is recalled for further examination."

I have also been approached by several representative Members of the Corporation and citizens as to the propriety of obtaining, on behalf of the Corporation, the counterpart of the proposed War Drawings and Sketches in France, viz:– Drawings and Sketches of Steel, Aeroplane and Munition Works in the City and in the Clyde Yards, including River scenes, so that these, like the French Sketches, should be added to the City's permanent Collection of Etchings and Black and White Drawings which we have started at our Art Galleries in Kelvingrove.

While the originals would, of course, become the property of the Corporation it has, subject to your sanction being given, been arranged that Mr. Farrell, the local Black and White Artist, and Dr. Neil Munro, the well-known Journalist and Writer, should jointly undertake and carry out the work, and should issue a volume, or it might be two volumes, titled "Glasgow and the Clyde during the Great War", and containing photogravure copies of the Sketches with some explanatory letterpress. The issue would be that of a limited edition; and such, like the Collection of Drawings and Sketches to be taken in France, would, I am satisfied, be highly appreciated and prized by the Corporation and by the general body of the people, and would together form a fitting official and pictorial history of the War, and of the War work of the City and Clyde.

In the circumstances I, on behalf of the Corporation make the request to you, as the Competent Military Authority, to grant sanction to Mr. Farrell and Dr. Munro to proceed with the proposed work and I confidently trust you will give the necessary permission.

In the copy letters sent you I have stated my opinion of Mr. Farrell and his personal and professional worth. I adhere to that opinion. You personally know Dr. Munro as well as I do; and I am sure that both of these gentlemen would take the greatest possible care to strictly observe any conditions that you or your Department might think fit to attach to the permission.

I am,
My Lord Marquess,
Yours very sincerely,
Thomas Dunlop
Encl.

Minutes of the Corporation of the City of Glasgow and Committees, 18 October 1917, Print No. 27, p. 2005, para c, in *Minutes of the Corporation of Glasgow, April 1917 to Nov 1917*, Glasgow Museums Archives.

There was submitted a letter, of date 17th instant, from Mr. Fred. A. Farrell, 185 Bath Street, Glasgow, intimating that, through the courtesy and interest of the Lord Provost and the Town-Clerk, he has been granted permits by the Ministry of Munitions and the Admiralty to compile a permanent record in drawings of some of the more outstanding phases of the war work being done in the City of Glasgow and on the Clyde; offering to present to the Corporation a selected fifty of the original drawings of the said work; as also, on the necessary permit being obtained, sketches of the work in France of the Highland Light Infantry and other battalions raised by the Corporation asking, as a condition of the gift, that he be allowed to retain the copyrights of the drawings for a period of five years after the signing of the peace terms, as during the period he would issue the complete records in the form of Editions de Luxe, limited in number, and suggesting that, if accepted, the drawings be taken over as 'The Sir Thomas Dunlop Collection of War Records,' as a tribute to the work and worth of Sir Thomas during his term of office as Lord Provost, and thereafter housed in the Art Galleries at Kelvingrove. The Corporation unanimously agreed to accept, on the condition mentioned, the generous and appropriate gift, and to instruct the Town-Clerk to convey to Mr. Farrell their grateful and appreciative thanks therefore.

'Glasgow Artist's War Sketches', *Glasgow Herald*, 7 November 1917, p. 6h.

By invitation of the War Office Mr. Fred A. Farrell, the well-known Glasgow etcher and black-and-white artist is leaving for France to make a series of drawings on the battle front for the Glasgow Corporation's permanent records of the war. He is also executing a series depicting national effort on the Clyde in connection with the war. These are to be included in the collection which is to be known as the Sir Thomas Dunlop War Records and to be placed in Kelvingrove Art Galleries.

Minutes of the Corporation of the City of Glasgow and Committees. At a special meeting of the Committee on Parks, Gardens & Galleries, 28 October 1918, Print No. 27, p. 2100, issued 11 November 1918, in *Minutes of the Corporation of Glasgow, April 1918 to Nov 1918*, Glasgow Museums Archives.

With reference to minute of the Corporation, of date 18th October, 1917 (Print No. 27, page 2005), when (1) there was submitted a letter, of date 17th *idem*, from Mr. Fred. A. Farrell, 185 Bath Street, intimating that, through the courtesy and interest of the Lord Provost and the Town-Clerk, he had been granted permits by the Ministry of Munitions and the Admiralty to compile a permanent record of drawings of some of the more outstanding phases of the war work being done in the city and on the Clyde; offering to present to the Corporation a selected fifty of the original drawings of the said work, as also, on the necessary permit being obtained, of sketches of the work in France of the Highland Light Infantry and other Battalions raised by the Corporation, and asking, as a condition, that he be allowed to retain the copyright of the drawings for a period of five years after the signing of the peace terms, as, during that period he would issue the completed records in the form of *editions de luxe*, limited in number, and suggested that, if accepted, the drawings be taken over as the "Sir Thomas Dunlop Collection of War Records", as a tribute to the work and worth of Sir Thomas during his term of office as

Lord Provost, and thereafter housed in the Art Galleries at Kelvingrove; and (2) the Corporation unanimously agreed to accept, on the conditions mentioned, the generous and appropriate gift, and instructed the Town-Clerk to convey to Mr. Farrell their grateful and appreciative thanks therefore, the chairman read a letter, of date 26th current, addressed to him by Mr. Farrell, explaining that, in making the offer, he was prepared to devote six months' work and make an expenditure of £100 thereunder; that, under the permit, he was only allowed three weeks in France, and returned with about thirty-five subjects, which, under the circumstances, could only be obtained in notes; that, thereon he had directed his attention to the war work in the city and on the Clyde, under the Munitions and Admiralty permits granted him, and than on both phases of the work he had spent twelve months, and is about half-way towards completion, and is already over his second £100 of expenses; that the Ministry of Information had, on 18th current, advised the Town-Clerk that they had sent a recommendation to the War Office that he (Mr. Farrell) be attached to the famous 51st Division as soon as possible, for a period of two months, in order that the city's records of the Front be completed, and that he may at any time be warned to proceed to France, which will entail a further expenditure of £100; that he would gladly bear the whole expense himself, but is finding it heavy, and asking whether the committee would care to give relief in the matter of expenses beyond his first £100, and also provide for the framing of the pictures to be selected by them.

The chairman explained that Mr. Farrell's first visit was to Flanders, being attached to the 15th, 16th, and 17th H.L.I., and that, during his forthcoming visit, he will be attached to the Gordons, the Black Watch, the Seaforths, the Argylls, &c., of the 51st Division.

The committee having considered the foregoing letter, and having regard to the whole circumstance of the case,

Agreed to recommend the Corporation to provide for the framing of the pictures in question, and to make a contribution of £200 to Mr. Farrell towards the expenses referred to by him, payment of that amount to be made as follows, viz.: – (1) the sum of £100 when Mr. Farrell receives the necessary permit from the War Department to proceed to France; and (2) the sum of £100 when the Corporation select and take possession of the fifty drawings gifted to them – Councillor McMillan dissenting.

(Approved by the Corporation on 31st October, 1918 – See page 2064 hereof.)

'The 51st Division: War Drawings by Mr. Fred Farrell', *Glasgow Herald*, **30 April 1920, p. 8h.**

The war drawings upon which Mr. Fred Farrell has been engaged for two and a half years are now completed, and are to be reproduced in a volume on "The 51st Division," with an introduction by Mr. Neil Munro, LLD, which is to be published this summer. Mr. Farrell, who enjoys a considerable reputation as an etcher, was commissioned to make drawings at the front for the Corporation of Glasgow, the only city which was granted permits for the purpose. The aim of the artist has been to record the great war in two of its phases, the life and activities of the men at the front, and the work of the women in the shell factories. He was attached to the 51st Highland Division, and his pictorial survey ranges from Albert in the south to Langemarck in the north, and from the Kemmel-Arras line in the west to the Cambrai-Valenciennes line in the east. The eighty odd drawings from the front, scarcely form a spectacular pageant of war. But that was not Mr. Farrell's purpose. Modern warfare, as he describes it, "is a work-a-day business for officers and men", and in that spirit he approached his formidable task. The results are, however, by no means prosaic. Mr. Farrell's records are punctiliously exact, in respect of their transcripts of the landscape in the war area, as of the character and equipment of the men engaged. Authoritative descriptions of the officers and men represented accompany each of the drawings. They are records of actuality, and legitimately come within the category of historical documents. In all of them Mr. Farrell's fine sense of artistry is manifest. Whether his medium be black and white, or colour tint, he is always convincing. In the set of munition sketches, of which there are two dozen, he renders a mass of detail with great skill, his subjects ranging from the rough turning of a shell to the forging of a big gun. The character of the industrial side of war is eloquently expressed, and the drawings also suggest the poetry that lurks in the noisy environment of shipyard and factory. The drawings were displayed yesterday in the Banqueting Hall of the City Chambers, and made impressive appeal as a pictorial chronicle of war. Under agreement Mr. Farrell presents fifty of them to the Corporation, but it is to be hoped that the remainder may be purchased for the municipal collection. Added to the fact that they are the work of one of the most promising of the younger artists of Glasgow, the drawings form a record, the only one of its kind outside London.

Fred A. Farrell, Chelsea Arts Club, 143 Church Street, S.W. to Sir John Lindsay, 24 April 1919, Glasgow Museums Archives, GMA.2014.1.2.

Dear Sir John,

I am sorry I did not see you before leaving for London where I shall get the War Records finished.

The holiday week-end upset my calculations and on Tuesday I had to work hard at packing but was hoping to make a visit and say goodbye when I was told you were out of town.

Here I shall finish the Records in the shortest possible time.

There are forty framed subjects in the Studio at 104 West George Street. If Mr. Brotchie can give these safe storage as requested by you could you ask him to communicate with me and I could have them sent to the Galleries under his care?

I trust you are well and beg you to accept my kindest regards.

Believe me,
Yours sincerely,
Fred A. Farrell.

Over: *South Portal, Ypres Cathedral* (detail), dated December 1917.

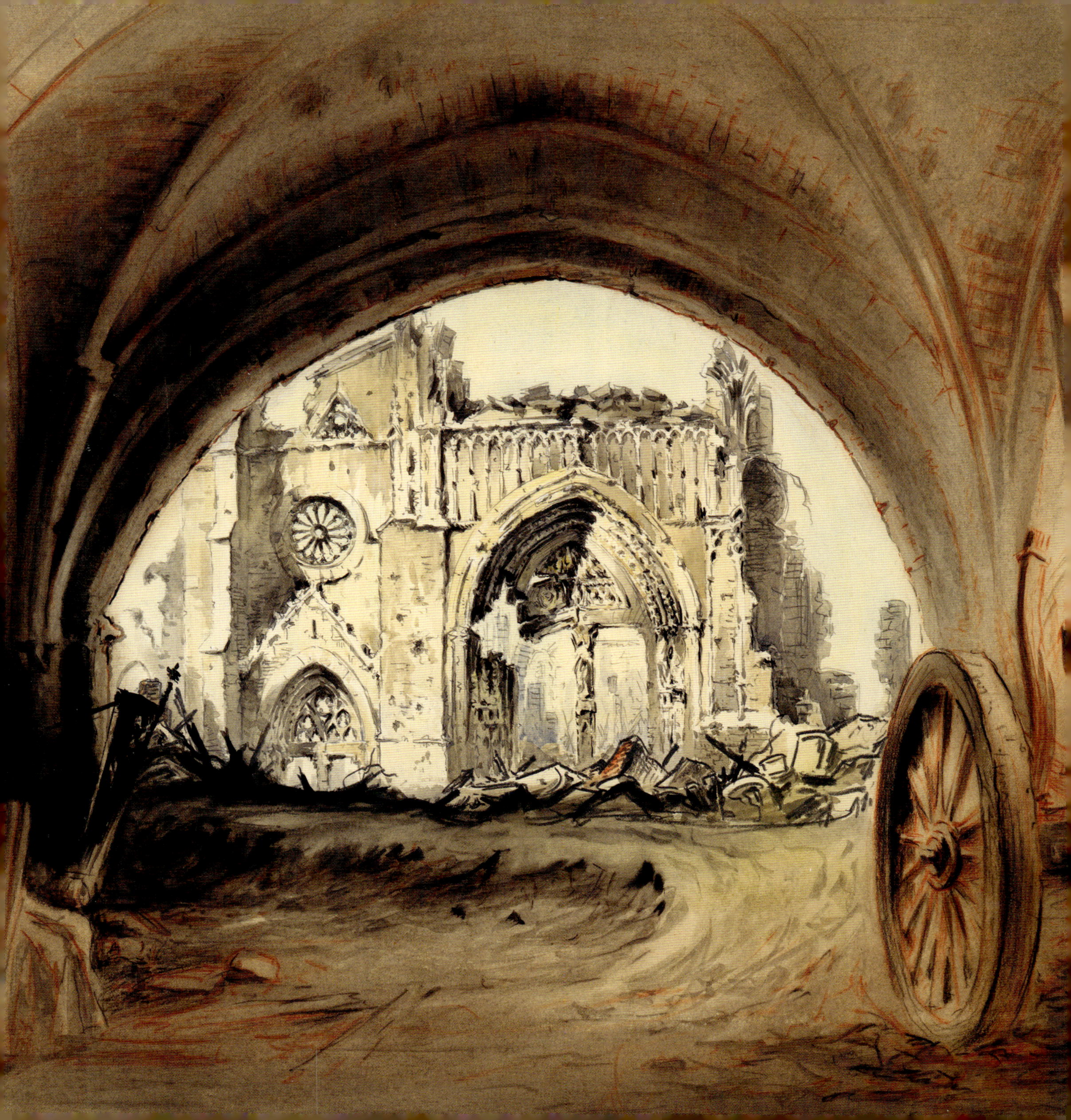